Operating in the Fulfillment
of
Divine Purpose

**Fulfilling divine purpose is a spiritual journey that
must be completed in a physical body**

Mark E. Crutcher, Ph.D.

PRESS

Operating In The Fulfillment Of Divine Purpose
by Dr. Mark E. Crutcher

Printed in the United States of America

ISBN 9781613794647

www.xulonpress.com

To Pastor Rick Jackson

Be Blessed in God

(M<unclear>c</unclear>) 1/4/12

Dedication

This book is dedicated to my wife, Juanita M. Crutcher, whom God gave unto my life. I want you to know that you bring inspirations and blessings to my life. I thank God for bringing us together in a manner that helps both of us to fulfill His purpose for our lives. Please know that I have loved you from the moment I saw you, and I will always love you.

You came into my life when I was attempting to answer God's call as a servant leader, and you brought balance and love into a life that needed it. God has used you to help me become the servant and leader that I am today. Together we have touched so many people who were looking for God in the relationship between a man and his wife.

Thank you for your love and for being a wonderful mother for our children and for many other children who needed a mother. Thank you for not being too selfish to share your husband with the work of God and being willing to work with him to fulfill God's will. Thank you for the sacrifices you have made for our family, our love, and our service to God.

Know that your love continues to be an extension of God's love to keep me warm in an often cold world, comforted in a sometimes lonely world. Thank you for your love, friendship, and loyalty in the covenant relationship that we share with each other and God.

Table of Contents

Preface

A Latin American I know tells the story of how his father spent thirty years trying to sneak into America and got sent back to Mexico every time. Finally his father went to an immigration attorney and discovered that his father was born in Texas, which made him a U.S. citizen already. This man spent a large portion of his life trying to become what he already was.

Do you know why you exist? Why you are here on this planet called earth? What was God up to when He fashioned you?

Destiny can be defined as the predetermined reason for your existence in the experience we call life. Fulfillment of that destiny involves personal choices, revelations, and life events that affect the course of your life. Ironically, one of the most prominent events that can affect your destiny is the *lack of knowledge* of your divine purpose in life. Because God made you with a specific design, you should be aware that He had a purpose in giving you life and gifts to function through life.

Purpose can be defined as the reason that a person or thing exists and relates to what is expected of the creation. Since God made everyone and all things, it should be important to discover what God was up to in giving you existence. If you were created by God with specific thoughts, actions, and instructions, then you must have a specific purpose for existing. If you are unaware of that purpose, you might also be unaware of who you are. You also could be unaware of what belongs to you and what you are supposed to accomplish in life. You could spend a large amount of your time trying to be something that you were not designed to be or—like the Latin American man—trying to become what you already are.

As you journey through the pages of this book, ask God to send you revelations that help you understand why you exist. As you read, give prayerful reflection on your past, present, and future desires for clues about your purpose. Knowing the purpose God has for your life should help you to focus as you make decisions that will alter the course of your life. Such knowledge should also help you to avoid those situations and people who would take your life off course or disrupt your fulfillment process. It is my prayer that this book will help you discover and live your life *Operating in the Fulfillment of Divine Purpose*.

Introduction

Then God said, Let us make man in our image, according to our likeness and let them have dominion over the fish of the sea, over the birds of the air, and over the cattle, over all the earth and every creeping thing that creeps on the earth. So God created man in His image, in the image of God He created him, male and female He created them. Then God blessed them, and God said to them, be fruitful and multiply, fill the earth and subdue it; have dominion over the fish of the sea, over the birds of the air, and over every living thing that moves on the earth.

Genesis 1:26-28

The creation story makes it plain: humanity was created by God with a specific purpose and a specific design to carry out that divine purpose. God was specific in His thoughts about creating humans, specific in His action of creating humans, and specific in His instructions to created humans. But the first man and woman—these magnificent created beings who contained the very breath of God—lost their divine purpose through an act of rebellion and disobedience inspired by the deception of the serpent. The first humans found themselves separated from God and out of position to fulfill the divine purpose of their creation.

But then something wonderful happened. God began to reveal Himself in preparing humans for their reconciliation into His presence and will, which occurred through the sacrifice and victory of Jesus over sin and death. Since the fall of the first humans, humanity has been struggling to discover and fulfill its divine purpose given by the Creator.

This book examines two concepts of life and identifies five stages that are essential in the discovery and fulfillment of divine purpose. The two concepts of life that must be understood are *abiding in the presence of God* and *understanding demonic influence*. The five stages of divine purpose include:

- Discovery of Divine Purpose
- Acceptance of Divine Purpose
- Walking in Divine Purpose
- Fulfillment of Divine Purpose
- Testimony of Divine Purpose

This book also attempts to introduce and explain a major tool referred to as the Flaming Sword, which is available to believers in their attempt to fulfill God's purpose for their lives.

Unit 1
In His Presence

**Spiritual Principle: If you draw near to God,
He will draw near to you.**

Chapter 1

Spiritual Communion: Being with God

Humanity was created to abide in the presence of God with three main purposes in mind—spiritual communion, spiritual revelation, and spiritual impartation. All of these purposes are spiritual because God is a Spirit and created a universe where spiritual things *often unseen* affect the natural things that are seen. Much like the wind, which cannot be seen, has such a vast affect on the things of nature that can be seen. We can see things that are affected by the wind even when they are caught up in its power. Thus, we witness natural things that are affected by and caught up in the power of God. We must understand that we are spiritual beings living in natural bodies and allow our spiritual nature to affect our natural existence.

So what exactly is spiritual communion? Spiritual communion involves being connected and experiencing a sense of belonging— being one with God, a part of God, and sharing both life and existence with God. To commune with God means to be with Him both spiritually and naturally. This need for communion with God is illustrated in God's first recorded question to man, "Adam, where are you?" Given the facts that Adam and God were both in the garden and this is the first interaction between God and man after man's act of disobedience suggests a spiritual separation (death) between God and man. The separation brings the necessity for questions between

God and man and indicates a loss of communion and belonging. Man's action of covering, hiding, and fear also suggests a feeling of not belonging but alienation (Genesis 3:6-10).

While spiritual communion involves being with God, it also involves worship of God motivated by love and acceptance of His sovereignty. That which He created knows Him for who and what He is, bows in submission to His glory, and gives Him honor. Anything that knows God and refuses to give Him such honor takes on the nature of devils. Everything in the presence of God must worship Him. Through the communion of worship all created beings share existence, life, and purpose with God. Such worship is motivated by the love of God that abides within creation and is given by those who have hearts for God.

Jesus died and rose from the dead so that He could remove the alienation—essentially bridging the gap—between God and humanity. By doing so, He made it possible for humanity to enter the presence of God and *be* with God in spiritual purpose as well as in natural phenomena. Believers are committed to sharing existence, life, and purpose with God's will. The will, nature, and purpose of God can be expressed in all created things that are with Him. This is what it means to be Christlike (Christian), for God's desire for redemption, His love for creation, and His divine purpose to reconcile creation to Himself were all expressed in Christ.

Everything that is one with God is able to carry on a natural existence while exemplifying spiritual and supernatural expressions of God. In this sense, Jesus walked in the natural experiencing pain, rejection, and thirst, as well as in the supernatural expressing healing, acceptance, and resurrection. All created things that are with God can experience this type of life that has both natural and supernatural expressions. This is why Jesus said His disciples would be able to do greater works than His earthly miracles. This is not limited to humans only. Consider the burning bush that spoke the words of God to Moses without being consumed, the donkey who spoke God's warning and correction to Balaam, and the rocks that waited to cry out praises to the Lord. If created things are not with God, they become cursed like the fig tree that had leaves but produced no fruit, or the serpent who deceived Eve in the garden (Genesis 3:1-7).

While humans are not exclusive to the natural/supernatural existence, they are a part of the phenomenon if they are with God. Moses' face shined with the glory of God after being in His presence. Peter walked on the water with Jesus, and both Elijah and Paul raised the dead because it was the will of God. This natural/supernatural reality exists because God occupies everything that is with Him in life and purpose. These things become an extension of God through which He expresses His will, nature, and purpose, just as the burning bush spoke God's will in directing Moses to lead Israel out of Egypt and bondage. The ground around the bush became holy because the bush turned into an extension of God.

Whatever God occupies with His presence becomes holy like the Ark of the Covenant (2 Samuel 6:12-15) or the disciples on the Day of Pentecost (Acts 2:1-4). God's anointing abides in His presence and gives authority to whatever or whoever He possesses over the forces of evil and death. The ark was a wooden box made by the hands of men with manmade engraving on the outside. This is how the ark appeared to the enemies of Israel, but when the heathen nation stole it, it became a holy manifestation of the power of God to defeat the enemy. When the ark was placed in the enemy's camp, their idol statue was destroyed by the presence of God in the ark. The idol could not stand or prevail because the Spirit of God occupied the Ark of the Covenant and made it a holy extension of God.

As believers we must be with God in life and purpose so that He can abide with us and express His supernatural presence in our lives. The supernatural expressions of God's presence enable believers to transcend the natural laws and experience miraculous occurrences for the benefit of the kingdom of God. It is through this connection that believers become more than conquerors and are able to "do all things through Christ Jesus." On the Day of Pentecost Peter became a living witness of the supernatural presence of God operating in a natural vessel. He was willing to put his life on the line for the purpose of God, and the world witnessed the transformation of fearful, denying Peter into a passionate orator who inspired three thousand souls to be saved on that day.

The enemy of humanity, Satan, realizes that through the presence of God humanity is able to overcome the natural hindrances to spiritual communion with God and each other. Satan knew that once separated from God, humanity would drift apart from each other due to impure thoughts and motives. Therefore, he began early to cause separation between God and humanity and each other. Satan initiated his attack on marriage and family to prevent humanity from being in a state that God can occupy in spiritual communion and express His supernatural presence.

Separation from God

Humanity fell into sin through the actions of the first humans and became spiritually dead or separated from God. In Genesis 2:17 God warns Adam that he will surely die if he eats of the tree of the knowledge of good and evil. Genesis 3:6 informs us that Adam and Eve ate of the forbidden tree. Sin manifested itself in the lives of the first humans, and in that one act all of humanity entered into the state of sin. In this state humanity exists in death because sin disrupted the relationship, communion, and fellowship with God. The curse began when sin manifested itself in the lives of Adam and Eve. At that very moment they became dead (separated from God) and began to show signs of shame and hide from each other behind manmade coverings; they also tried to hide from the presence of God behind the covering of nature.

Humans in their carnal nature are still hiding from each other behind manmade coverings of society that give social status. We are ashamed to reveal ourselves because we inherited the cursed nature of the first humans. Without the cursed nature, we would not have improper thoughts or actions toward someone. Because our spirit is surrounded with sinful flesh, we have to be aware and careful about impure thoughts and actions toward people we are not in covenant relationship with. Sometimes these impure thoughts cause us to feel ashamed because we know they are inappropriate. For instance, we may take too much time interacting with someone of the opposite sex, especially when we find them attractive and realize we have gone out of our way to be extra nice and attentive. A friend once told me that an attractive young lady was praising him for being such a righteous man of God. He walked away from the conversation repenting because of the improper thoughts he had just experienced about the young lady.

The carnal nature of humanity can also affect our motives when interacting with family members, people in the workplace, and even in the service of God. We have to prevent our carnal natures from tainting our motives of service. Sometimes our humanism causes us to serve for selfish reasons rather than for the glory of God. Because of the cursed nature we can even get caught up in self-exaltation and disobedience when we mean to serve God. Moses and Aaron were victims of the carnal nature when they struck the rock and proclaimed they were giving the Israelites water rather than obeying and honoring God (Numbers 20:1-13).

Our shame results from the cursed nature we inherited from Adam and Eve. Therefore, we are subject to the lust of the eye, the lust of the flesh, and the pride of life. This is the same sin illustrated in Genesis 3:6 and 1 John 2:15-17. All sin can be placed in one of these three categories of temptation. In the sin state we have the capacity of sin, which means that any act against God could manifest itself within our lives (Genesis 4:7). It is through our impure thoughts and motives that the enemy attempts to twist even our actions of good intent into something sinful or harmful to the children of God.

Adam and Eve did not fully understand their relationship with God, and so the serpent easily convinced them they were lacking something when all of their needs were fulfilled in God. They had no need of the knowledge they were seeking as long as they remained dependent on God. Because their actions would be guided by His love, they would automatically walk into the way of righteousness. It was only when they decided they needed to know good and evil for themselves that they began the journey that would lead them away from God. Their sin began when they decided to try to become independent of God. In following the suggestions of the serpent, they sought knowledge separate from God. By taking this course of action, they made the statement that God was not providing for all their needs and so they took matters into their own hands. In allowing their minds to be seduced by Satan, they took on a part of the nature of Satan, who chose to be independent of God and also desired to be God.

The devil has used this old trick throughout the ages. He tries to deceive us that we are lacking and need to take matters into our own hands rather than trust God to fulfill all of our needs. Upon receiving the fruit from the tree of knowledge, Adam and Eve's eyes were fully opened. The first evil they came to know was within themselves. They were ashamed to be fully open with each other [naked] (Genesis 3:7) and ashamed to be in the presence of God (Genesis 3:8).

When we break the sanctity of our relationships with each other and with God, we find it difficult, if not impossible, to be fully open with one another. These acts prevent us from full disclosure and create a separation in our relationships. In the separated state, we are not able to fully touch and agree with the person God placed in our lives to help us fulfill His purpose for our lives. Before eating from the tree, Adam and Eve did not have a disclosure problem. The Bible says they were naked and not ashamed (Genesis 2:25 KJV) and gives no indication they were ashamed of each other or of being in the presence of God. This kind of separation can occur in all types of relationships where the trust level has been broken or seriously damaged.

Freedom to Choose

Humanity was created with free will, which enabled them to make choices about their existence. Free will was a part of their state of being, received from the Creator who is absolute being. This free will state of being was not designed to operate in independence from God but rather as a state of being in God. In exercising their sense of being, Adam and Eve made a choice. However, they looked to the wrong source of inspiration for guidance in making that choice. This choice separated them from God due to their disobedience. The sin of independence is illustrated in the story of Adam and Eve (Genesis 3:5 KJV) and also in the account of God's people at the tower of Babel (Genesis 11:3-4 KJV).

The lure of the tree of knowledge seemed to offer freedom, but instead it offered captivity, shame, and alienation. Humanity was dependent upon God before their fall from grace and existed in ultimate freedom. Being subject to God frees humanity from the influences of evil (death, sickness, pain, hunger, need, etc.) Humanity was designed to be bound to God and not independent, for God even restricted Himself to His Word and to His people. If God, who is pure, holy, and righteous, found it wise to tie Himself to something then we humans who are born in sin should take notice of the need to be bound to God. If we are not subject to God we become subject to evil spirits that influence the selfish nature of humanity inherited from the first humans.

While discussing the Sunday school lesson one morning, a recently married brother made a statement to the group of men in the class that really drove this point home. He said that he had bound himself to one woman and it freed him from the influence of all other women. He expressed how his act of binding himself to a woman in the manner that God instituted enabled him to be free of forces that once influenced his life. We should take this same approach in our relationship with God; if we are bound to God, it looses us from being bound to Satan and his influences. Our bond with God frees us from the evil forces that attempt to bind us to a life of sin and unrighteousness.

Humanity's reach for "freedom" left a void due to the separation from God and room for contrary spirits to abide in the vessels of humans (Matthew 12:43-45). Even in society, we can only have freedom by binding ourselves to a social contract referred to as the law. The law creates the boundaries of relationships and binds us to a social contract that helps to regulate our selfish natures. A society without a social contract abides in chaos and becomes subject to the selfish natures of the whole of society. In such a society, everyone becomes a slave to the independent spirits that prey on the unregulated, unbound fleshly nature of humanity. Societies with laws seem to function better and their people enjoy more freedoms.

Living in Sin

When we understand that separation is death, we become aware that the sin nature of the flesh causes us to move into death. Such movement into death (separation) causes us to bring the spirit of death (separation) into our relationships with God and with each other. The act of spreading death is illustrated in Genesis 4:3-12

(NKJV) in the story of Cain and Abel. In this biblical account, early humans brought offerings in an attempt to worship God even before the dispensation of the Law. The spirit within humanity seeks to be reunited and in communion with God and recognizes a need for atonement.

The story of Cain and Abel also illustrates the flaws within fallen humanity and the desire of sin to rule over humanity. However, in Genesis 4:7 (KJV) God informs Cain that he should rule over sin, which is similar to Jesus' statement to Peter in Luke 22:31 that Satan desired to sift him like wheat, but Jesus had prayed for him that his faith would not fail. When we are being sifted by the forces around us, we must remind ourselves that Jesus has prayed for us to hold on to our faith. The sifting only separates (kills) the chaff (unrighteousness) from the wheat (that which does the will of God in our lives). God allows our sifting so that we are able to rule over the sin nature of the flesh. Remember, Peter was able to stand on the Day of Pentecost after being sifted and confirm the presence of the Holy Spirit in the lives of the disciples of Christ. Through Jesus we are given power over the forces of sin that operate in our lives.

Notice in the story of Cain and Abel how early the sin nature ruled over humanity. The first man born in sin murdered the second man born in sin, his brother. The sin nature ruled over Cain and brought death between himself and Abel and between himself and God. Cain demonstrated the capacity to sin in his interaction with God and his brother. He also felt shame and attempted to hide behind sarcasm in his dialogue with God. This sin nature (death and separation) prevents true worship of God. This precept becomes even more profound when we recognize that a *living* spirit is required to worship the true and living God. It is necessary to be in the presence of God to truly worship Him. For this reason, in the dispensation of the Law, God allowed the high priest to represent Israel and meet Him in the Most Holy Place behind the veil as recorded in Leviticus 16.

During the dispensation of the Law, humanity was separated from God and a veil was erected across the entrance of the Most Holy Place, where the presence of God met humanity (Exodus 25:22). God abided in the Most Holy Place, and the veil served as a divider between the Holy Place and the Most Holy Place, which divided the sinful nature of man from the presence of God. The sinful nature of humanity made it necessary for the veil to be erected because God abides in holiness and sin disrupts the communion with God. As we move toward sin, our own feelings, emotions, fears, and desires form a veil that separates us from the presence of God. Just as the veil of the temple was erected by humanity, we form the separation that occurs between us and God. Even though God is near us, our sins cause us to feel distant from Him. Adam and Eve experienced this feeling of isolation after their act of disobedience and demonstrated it by hiding from God.

The separation of humanity prevents the true worship God desires where His worshipers abide in His presence and exemplify His nature of holiness, righteousness, and love. As we seek to worship God, we must draw near to Him and exemplify His nature so that we can enter into His presence and touch Him. We cannot accomplish this on our own due to the sinful nature of humanity. The inherited sin nature that was passed from Adam is known as original sin. There is also the learned sin nature that we commit in our mortal bodies known as actual sin (Romans 5:12). These two sin natures work in humanity and hinder any attempt to draw near to God and exemplify Him. Therefore, humanity is also hindered from truly worshiping God and fulfilling the divine purpose of creation.

Bridging the Gap

The separation from God due to the sinful nature of humanity made it necessary for God to send Jesus into the world to save humanity. John 3:16 instructs us that God was motivated by love to send Jesus into the world of humanity. Therefore, Jesus is the ultimate expression of God's love toward humanity. Romans 5:6-11 illustrates that God reconciled us through the death of His Son Jesus (brought us back to Him). This act of God's love is able to cancel out the sinful nature of humanity and reconcile us back to God. This act also ushered in the dispensation of grace into the world of humanity. Romans 5:18-21 instructs us that through Jesus the offense is taken away and grace, which is a free gift, is given to humanity.

The act of God's love through Jesus Christ allowed humanity to have access to God the Father. Through Jesus, humanity is able to abide in the presence of God and engage in true worship of God. We are born again spiritually as we accept Jesus as our Savior. This new birth enables us to become the children of God, and as children we are no longer far away from God. Being brought near and in the presence of God, we are able to be one with Him. True worship requires the touching of and agreement with God. The touching is being one with God to the point where He becomes a part of us and we become part of Him. This is why Jesus said, "My father and I are one because I am in the Father and the Father is in me. Through Jesus we are able to live in agreement with God and experience spiritual communion with the Father.

Being in agreement with God refers to humanity taking on the nature of God. As we draw close to Him we enter into His presence, His very essence of holiness, righteousness, and love. In His presence, we are transformed as we take on His nature and become more like Him and less like the world. This transformation allows us to operate in the purposes of God as we conduct ourselves according to His will. We are able to overcome natural tendencies and desires that attempt to rule over us.

In answering the call of God into ministry, I realized certain habits in my life were contrary to God's Word and would hinder the work of ministry. In order to answer the call, I had to draw closer to God, and this closeness transformed my life. I found that many of the things that had once negatively influenced my actions began to lose their power over me. I remember talking to a friend one year at our college homecoming, and another friend overheard our conversation and came up to me saying he could tell I had changed just from my response during the discussion. I agreed with him that God's influence in my life had caused changes in my behavior since we left college. When I asked him "Was I that bad?" his response was "Yes." This conversation helped me to recognize that a sincere desire to be transformed into the ways of righteousness is possible when we surrender to the presence and nature of God. As our desire moves into agreement with God's word, we become more in agreement with God, and this agreement gives us power to stay in the will of God and overcome the influences of the world.

Imitators of God

As we walk in agreement with God, we begin to desire the things of God, which enables Him to work through us—and we become imitators of Him (Ephesians 5:1 NIV). This is when we are able to speak the things that are not as though they were (Romans 4:17). Because of our agreement with God, we can discern the things of God, for the things that we speak of are not present in this world but they are in God. It's supernatural. We speak them into this world because the God that is within us knows they are needed and releases them through us. Because God always agrees with God, His power brings those things from the spiritual realm into the physical world of humanity. It is in this surrendered state that God can give us the desires of our heart, because our heart desires the things of God.

If we are to be imitators of God, it is important that we learn to speak the things of God, because He is a God who speaks things into being. He releases what is within Him in the spirit realm into whatever reality it needs to be manifested. In order to speak the things of God, it is important to know the language of God. To learn the language of God, we must study God's Word and allow the Holy Spirit to interpret the true nature of the Word. God's Word is written in the languages of humanity, but the Word is much more than what is on the pages. The Word is designed to give humanity revelations of God and His will for creation, through the working of the Holy Spirit. First Corinthians 2:9-14 inform us that the natural man cannot receive the things of God because they are spiritual. But because of Jesus' act of reconciliation, we are able to receive the things of God through the Holy Spirit.

Chapter 2

Spiritual Revelation

Humanity was created to receive spiritual revelations of God, which enables us to be like God. Because humans were designed in the image and likeness of God, we were created to be like God through God-given revelations. It is amazing how Satan offered to humanity what God would already give them according to His will (1 John 3:2). Through the craftiness of the serpent, Satan tempted humanity to try to understand God and the purpose of creation on their own. In following Satan's advice humanity lost much of what belonged to them. Sin caused mankind to be deformed and lose knowledge of God, but God has been revealing Himself to humans since creation (Romans 1:18-23). Through spiritual revelations God shares awareness and understanding of His presence, His nature, and His will for creation. If believers are united with God in life and purpose then these God-given spiritual revelations will transform them, causing redeemed humanity to emulate the divine nature of God.

The transformation of being like God can occur as a physical phenomenon, such as Moses' face shining after being in the presence of God (Exodus 34:29-30) or the tongues of fire that sat on the disciples' heads on Pentecost (Acts 2.3). The supernatural existence of God expressed through nature is known as the Shekinah glory. This phenomenon is also expressed in the burning bush experience in which the bush burned but was not consumed. The bush became holy causing the ground around it to become holy, thereby affecting the actions of Moses.

As children of God and followers of Christ we need to become God's burning bush at some point in our lives. By revealing Himself through the bush, God was able to share His purposes with Moses. Like the burning bush, we are able to receive revelations of God in a manner that transforms our environment. As the glory of God is reflected through us it causes others to notice and turn aside from their personal ambitions and desires to seek and experience life-transforming experiences with God.

The revelations of God can also be found in a spiritual phenomenon such as Jesus' expression of being in the Father and the Father being in Him (John 14:8-21). The Word of God teaches that Jesus, who was born of a woman (son of man), was the express image of the Father (the Christ). Therefore, Jesus existed as both divine and natural, God and human in the same body. This dual existence is offered to humanity and can be achieved through belief, love, and obedience in Jesus Christ. Such revelations come through the Holy Spirit and transform our spiritual existence to reflect the presence, power, and nature of God. In this transformation others are able to experience the attributes of God through believers. This spiritual process allows us to become Christlike and reflect the image of God to transform the world around us.

Just as the ground became holy around the burning bush, the environment around us becomes holy as we are holy. The world becomes more conducive to the presence of God, and He is able to share more of His existence with mankind. Through the church, God shares revelations that create an atmosphere in which His presence can abide, His power transforms, and His nature is reflected.

If we as believers are to fulfill the divine purpose of our lives, it is important for us to be able to hear the heart of God. In hearing the heart of God we understand some of what God is up to in our lives and in the kingdom of God. In hearing the heart of God we are able to make righteous decisions, speak the things of God into existence, and position ourselves to receive the blessings needed to serve Him in the fullest. In order for us to hear the heart of God we must learn to agree with God through the knowledge of His Word, the connectivity of His Spirit, and the power of His love. It is important for us to spend time with God in meditation, worship, study, fellowship, and service as the early church did (Acts 2:40-47).

The Knowledge of God's Word

The Holy Scriptures reveal three major attributes of God's nature: He is omnipotent (*all-powerful*), omnipresent *(everywhere)*, and omniscient (*all-knowing*). This is the continuum of God that Christians refer to as the Trinity. The Scriptures illustrate this continuum as the Father, the Word (Jesus), and the Holy Spirit existing and operating as one and being one. While all of the attributes are present in all three persons of the Trinity, each of the persons seems to be responsible for one of these attributes.

God's Word makes Him all-knowing because all truth comes from God's Word. Even the knowledge shared by the spirit of the tree of knowledge of good and evil originated from the Word of God, for the tree was created by the Word. The knowledge was shared outside of God's will and only partly disseminated. For this cause man did not receive the wisdom of the Word, which reveals how to use knowledge in the righteousness of God. God's Word contains knowledge (knowing the things of God); wisdom (using knowledge for the righteousness of God); and understanding (awareness of the relationships of the things of God). God through His Word knows all things because they were created by His Word. He that created all things knows all things because He knows what they were created to be. Therefore, God's Word allows Him to be omniscient or all-knowing.

The Connectivity of the Spirit

The Spirit of God makes Him omnipresent or everywhere. God's Spirit allows Him to transcend all natural realities and be in all places at the same time. This same Spirit is present in all three persons of the Trinity, and He is able to fill everything that was created. The study of matter reveals that everything was created with space, and space was designed to be filled. Therefore, nothing exists that God cannot occupy. A physical God would be limited in traveling throughout creation, but God is a Spirit and able to fill all things.

The Spirit of God gives life to the things created by the Word of God and gives animation to them. This is why all things move and have their being in God, for He is the substance from which all things were made. This is the same power that made man become a living soul and separated him from the rocks, trees, and animals God created. This is where God shared His sense of being with humanity so that we could be the children of God.

Humanity was designed to commune with the Spirit of God, and this connectivity is what allows a natural, finite, and sinful human to connect with a spiritual, infinite, and holy God. We were designed to allow the Spirit of God to dwell within us and enable us to become more than flesh and blood, for we are not only human if we are in God and God is in us. Because what animates us and give us life is a part of the Spirit of God, a connective bond exists between God and humanity that allows us to transcend our natural state of existence. This connectivity allows God to transcend the natural laws of existence and abide within all of creation at the same time.

The Power of God's Love

The love of God comes from the Father, and it is what makes Him omnipotent or all-powerful. The Word of God contains creation power, and the Spirit of God gives life to creation, but the love of God is the force that enables the Word and the Spirit to operate. Love is the motivating force behind all that God does and fuels His will and existence. First John 4:16 informs us that God is love. Therefore, love is the power that makes Him God. This scripture also tells us that God loves us, and this love is illustrated in God sharing of Himself that all might exist. The love is also illustrated in God sending His only begotten Son (God becoming man) to die for all of us (John 3:16).

Love is the most powerful force in the universe. The Scriptures teach us that there abides faith, hope, and love, and the greatest of these is love (1 Corinthians 13:13). Love enables us to destroy the enemy. Love can end wars, prevent hunger, and bring all creation into the oneness of God. Love is the only force that can truly conquer the world, and it does not require guns, bombs, and other weapons of mass destruction. Our love for each other is what identifies us as belonging to God (1 John 3:19). In order to agree with God we must agree in love and thereby abide in Him and He in us (1 John 4:16).

Love is truly why Christ said that He and the Father were one, because the same love that abides in the Father abides within Him (the sharing of oneself that others may live). Christ had enough love in Him to overcome the death within us. He used the power of love to shed off our sins and rise from the dead. In Jesus we saw the love of God operating in humanity, and that love enabled humanity to transcend the state of sin and death. After our redemption He gave us the new commandment of love. To love God with all our heart, soul, and mind and to love our neighbor as ourselves are the greatest commands God ever gave us. The entire law of God is fulfilled in these two commandments of love.

As God shares revelations of Himself with humanity, His believers are able to exemplify His attributes of knowledge, connectivity, and love. The sharing process is God's way of transforming humanity's environment. Through love humans are able to become aware of the type of existence God planned for us and to understand how to change our environment. When God's nature is revealed to humans we also receive revelations about His holiness and righteousness.

Because love involves giving ourselves to God, it is the process through which humans become holy. Being holy means belonging to God in purpose and life. Therefore, the giving of ourselves, our possessions, and the things we cherish to God develops a sense of belonging between us and God. God teaches us how to express His holiness in our daily lives. God is holy and He requires that we be holy as well. The holiness of God is expressed through those who live surrendered lives, reflecting the purpose of God in glorifying Him and edifying His kingdom. The revelations of God teach believers how to bring all things into subjection to God and allow His presence to manifest. God manifests His presence in what belongs to Him in life and purpose, but He will not dwell in whatever rebels against His purpose (John 14.23-24).

Jesus' sacrifice made it possible for the presence of God to abide within us. In submission to the presence of God, believers become holy and accessible to the presence and purpose of God. As believers, we abide in the world but are not of the world because we belong to God. We become conduits by which God reveals His presence and nature to those we influence. We become God's burning bush through which He reflects His righteousness into the world. When we submit to the presence of God we abide in His righteousness and allow others to experience the natural agreeing with the divine supernatural.

Expressing God's Attributes

God reveals righteousness to believers so that we learn to walk in submission and obedience to His will and purpose. By sharing His righteousness with us, God allows us to release the spirit of obedience among humanity, which helps people to make the right choices in life. Our acts of righteousness are motivated by our love for God and designed to give glory to Him and keep us in His presence. We can remain in His presence and teach others to do so by acting like the God that is revealed to us. We become God's burning bush to the people in our lives. Through our acts of righteousness, we allow the light of God's glory to be revealed to the world around us (Matthew 5:16).

Through spiritual revelations we also express God's love. The Bible teaches us that to love is to know God. Therefore, we can't know Him or be born of Him without loving Him and each other (1 John 4:7-11). As believers we express God's love through our acts of compassion toward each other, our obedience to Him, and our worship of Him. God has revealed Himself as a loving God and taught us to love Him and each other. Through our expressions of God's most powerful attribute (love) we can help transform our environment to reflect the presence and purpose of God.

Chapter 3

Spiritual Impartation: Receiving from Him

S piritual impartation occurs when we enter the presence of God to receive favor and the manifestation of divine gifts from God. We are blessed so that we may become a blessing to others and share those blessings with the kingdom of God. Believers are called to receive and operate in the gifts that God has for our lives. Because all blessings come from God, it is necessary to enter into His presence to receive these gifts and transfer them into the lives of others. If we try to engage our spiritual gifts outside of the presence and purpose of God we become demonic in nature like Adam and Eve in their garden experience. For us to receive impartation or to impart into others, we must operate in the presence of God because He is the only one who can make the transference holy.

Like Abram, who entered into the presence of God through his obedience to leave his country to be blessed, we must walk into the obedience God has for our lives. In His presence God activates the spiritual gifts He placed within us at our creation. This activation allows us to operate in the favor of God, putting us in blessed positions, gaining righteous influence, acquiring needed resources, and accomplishing godly tasks. We become blessed of God and He transforms our surroundings with favor according to His will. Joseph experienced such favor when he was thrown in a pit, sold into slavery, and placed in prison. Each of these places became blessed because of the presence of God who was with Joseph.

As we become blessed by God, He transforms the state of our surroundings in our favor, according to His divine will. This occurs because God uses what He created to bless what He made and to complete His work. We are allowed to operate out of the abundant overflow of our lives for the good of God's kingdom. God blessed David with favor so that He could bless Israel through him, and David's major sin occurred when he used that favor to the harm of Uriah for the temptation of Bathsheba. It is important that we overcome our personal temptations so that God can use us to transform the environment in the lives of people to His pleasure.

The fallout of David's sins—including the death of his first child with Bathsheba, and the rebellion of his son Absalom—demonstrates how our sinful actions can bring harm to ourselves and others. However, it is important to know that God forgave David and used him in spite of his sins to transform lives to the glory of God. Though he was forgiven, David caused great harm to the people around him and the kingdom of Israel. This is why it is so important for us to avoid fleshly desires that are subject to demonic influences. The Bible instructs us to submit unto God and resist the devil, and he will flee from us.

Through our blessedness, God is able to transform the environment and lives of people in our sphere of influence. Such manifestations of God are designed to make the people and situations we influence acceptable to the presence and purpose of God (holy). Through us God transforms our environment to His will and pleasure so that it reflects His nature. Sickness is healed, poverty is diminished, death is changed to life, and weakness is made into strength. Supernatural impartations are transferred through us from the presence of God to transform the world to His honor (Ephesians 3:20).

When we belong to God in life and purpose, He inhabits us to do His pleasure, as conduits through which His presence and nature are revealed to humanity. One Sunday morning a bird flew into the sanctuary of our church and alighted on the altar rail. Someone tried to catch the bird, but it flew away, circled around, and came back to land on the altar rail once more. I was standing in the rear of the

33

church when God spoke to me and said, "Go get the bird." I walked up the center aisle praying for God's presence. When I arrived at the altar rail, I reached out and picked up the bird. The bird did not fly, squawk, or even squirm as I placed my hands around it. I carried it to the door and released it. God had me tell the congregation that my hands became God's hands at that moment when I picked up the bird. Therefore, the bird knew the hands of its Creator, and sensing the presence of God within me the bird was at peace. Through me and the bird, God demonstrated the power of His presence that day to all of us in the house.

As followers of God we must keep His presence active in our lives to the point that it can be demonstrated through us. The active presence of God is often associated with fire because fire has the power to change the form of matter and give off energy as heat and light. As believers we often encourage each other to keep the fire burning on the altar of our hearts. We refer to the presence of God that can be seen by the world and has the power to transform the things within its influence.

Fire on the Altar

God is said to be a consuming fire (Hebrews 12:29), and the Bible documents many accounts where His presence is represented by fire. God spoke to Moses from a burning bush, led the children of Israel with a pillar of fire, sent tongues of fire on the disciples' heads at Pentecost, and appeared to John with eyes like flames of fire on the Isle of Patmos. Fire is also associated with the judgment of God and His acts of cleansing and separating that which is holy from the unholy.

The prophet John proclaimed that Jesus would baptize with the Holy Spirit and with fire. As we become born again through acceptance of Jesus as our Lord and Savior, Jesus baptizes us with the cleansing fire of the Holy Spirit, which ignites a flame within our soul. This flame consumes the unrighteousness from our souls and burns as a beacon of God's love, faith, and hope on the altar of our hearts.

In the Old Testament, the temple priests kept fire burning on the altar day and night for the sacrifices of the people. The fire was not allowed to go out (Leviticus 6:8-13). Since we are the temple of God under the new covenant, God's altar is in our hearts (Romans 10:8-10). Jesus ignites the flame within our hearts at our spiritual baptism, and it must be kept burning and never go out (Acts 2:1-4). This fire represents the presence of God living within our souls and empowers us to become children of God (John 1:12-13).

This flame must be kept burning in our hearts so that we can be the light of the world (Matthew 5:14-16). Jesus promised to empower the church to light up the world for His glory. This spiritual flame empowers us to live as children of God because it is a part of God living within us (Romans 8:9-11). As the priest worked to keep the fire burning on the Old Testament altar, we must spiritually work in relationship with Christ to keep the fire burning on the altar of our hearts. The spiritual fire in our hearts burns brighter with our sacrifices of praise, service, and prayer to illuminate our lives and the lives of those we influence.

In a fire, the flames act in union with oxygen to transform matter from one form to another. In much the same way, believers must act in union with God and one another to transform the natural order of the world for the presence of God. Through the active presence of God, believers are able to work together in a manner that allows them to accomplish more together than separately. The enemy is aware of this fact and constantly tries to influence our thoughts, desires, and actions to create division and turmoil. Believers can draw strength from the cooperative nature that exists in the Godhead, or the Trinity.

Synergy

The Trinity—the Father, Word, and Holy Spirit—acts in three persons but are one. Each of these personalities of God has separate functions that work together for the fulfillment of the kingdom of God. The Father is the source of existence (being), and by sharing His being He enables humanity to have being. The Word of God is the creative power of God that called everything into existence. The Word became flesh and reconciled a holy God with fallen humanity by paying the sin debt. The Holy Spirit allows natural man to transcend the natural forces and laws in order to commune with a supernatural (spiritual) God.

The three personalities, though distinct, all possess the attributes of each other in that they are God. They are also united in their purpose for the fulfillment of the whole. This unity in life and purpose creates a synergy within the Godhead that allows God to be all-powerful, all-knowledgeable, and all-present.

God shared the attribute of synergy with humanity in the creation process, which gives humans the ability to unite in transcending natural limitations. When Pentecost fully came the disciples were all with one accord in one place. Unity is paramount in operating in the fullness of God. The Bible teaches us that where two or three touch and agree in Jesus' name, the presence of God is in their midst. Not that He will come, but that He is already there, for it is God that draws us to unite with God. Jesus said, "If I be lifted up, I'll draw everyone to me (John 12.32 KJV). The God that is in one agrees with the God in all believers, forming a spiritual union within the body of Christ. God always agrees with God; therefore, the God that lives within all who are present creates a synergy, the ability of the united parts to produce a greater output than they are able to produce separately.

As we examine Genesis 1:26, we discover that God was in agreement with God in the creation of humanity. This agreement took place between the Father, Word, and Holy Spirit. Such agreement within the believer allows the creative power of God to operate within him or her. The Spirit of God that lives within humanity is in agreement with the Word of God that we received within us. This agreement gives life to a dead soul as it reveals to us that Jesus is the Christ and Savior of the world. God told the prophet Joel that He would pour out His Spirit on all flesh (Joel 2:28). The Spirit of God abides within humanity and awaits the agreement with the Word of God that is received within humanity. Romans 10:14 teaches us that we must hear before we can believe. This agreement is the beginning of new life in the believer and grows as the believer receives more of the Word of God to agree with the Spirit of God within.

The relationship of the Spirit and the Word can be illustrated in the operation of a gas pilot light. The fire is always burning, but when the presence of gas is increased the tiny flame ignites into a blazing inferno that produces heat. You can't bake any bread with the pilot light, but turning up the gas creates enough energy to cause the bread to rise (increase) and brown (mature). Because of the agreement of the Holy Spirit and the Word of God, our sight is connected to our hearing. If you can't hear God's Word then you won't be able to see what God is doing in your life.

On the day of Pentecost those in the upper room heard the sound of the Spirit before they saw the fire of the Spirit (Acts 2:2). Faith in God gives us the vision to prevent us from perishing (Proverbs 29:18, John 3:16-18). Vision can be described as seeing glimpses of the fulfillment of God's will for our lives, or seeing what God is up to. Our faith gives us such vision, and our faith comes from hearing the Word of God (Romans 10:17). This hearing refers to receiving the Word through our actions of obedience (Romans 10:9-10). The book of James instructs us to be more than simply hearers of the Word; we are called to be doers of the Word, because faith (belief beyond sight) without works (corresponding actions) is dead (James 3:14-26). Our faith must be proclaimed by what we say and manifested by what we do.

Years ago one of the neighborhoods in the city where I lived became so terrible that people were afraid to go out after dark. People would say they had to be in before the nightshift came to work. Young men involved in gangs and drug activity conducted drive-by shootings and gang fights on a regular basis. These activities took place in a small area that had four jukes (not clubs) in a four-block area. The Lord inspired me to ask the church to march through the area in prayer by faith and allow the presence of God within us to permeate the area. The Spirit of the Lord enabled me to understand that the activities occurring in that area were contrary to the Word of God and not motivated by love; therefore they were not in agreement with the Spirit of God. When such disagreement occurs curses begin to abide, and consequently sin, death, and destruction thrive in such places.

The first time we met in the area to do our prayer march, it started to rain. However, the people said they came to march in the name of the Lord, and a little water was not going to stop them. We began to march in song and prayer, not knowing what God would do but believing that He would do something. Within three months all four of the jukes were closed, with one becoming an apartment, another a clothing store, another a restaurant, and the fourth a church. Later that year during Christmas, we took the children caroling in that same area at night. We had a wonderful time celebrating the transformation that God had manifested in the area. The Spirit of the Lord revealed that the door was opened for God to reclaim the area. God moved through the presence of the church operating in faith as we heard the Spirit's call and began to walk forth beyond what we could see.

The church's action created an agreement within the area between the Spirit and the Word of God. Together we initiated the power of God that was needed to transform the area from a place of sin and death to an area of life and peace. Our answer to the call was our pilot light, and our actions of walking, praying, and singing provided the gas that God used to ignite a flame of cleansing within the area. God has given the power of synergy to the body of Christ so that we can transform the world if we live in agreement with the Spirit of God.

Like the Trinity, the church must recognize that it is one body with many parts. Each of these parts has different functions and distinct attributes necessary to carry out those functions. The different parts must be able to transcend their particular function and see the function of the whole body. The different parts must also understand that they work for the fulfillment of the whole body. This is the reason Satan works hard 24/7 to bring schisms, discord, and disharmony within the body of Christ. He wants to disrupt the synergy that exists within the body to overcome the things of the world. This synergy is the power of God to overcome all things according to His will. This power abides according to the need and is able to deal with whatever hinders the will of God for our lives.

At Pentecost, the disciples of Jesus heard a sound from heaven. They saw the fire sit upon them, and they were all filled with the Holy Spirit (presence of God). They were then able to speak with the united language of the Spirit of God that brought understanding to all who heard their words. This reveals that through the diversity of the body of Christ there is a commonality and unity. Although the function of my head is different from the function of my feet, the same life-giving blood that flows within my head flows within my feet. Both the head and the feet are designed to serve in unison within the body. Therefore, the diversity of the body of Christ is designed to serve the union of the body. The feet are not in competition with the head unless the body is dying. If we are to live we must learn to function in unison within the body of Christ.

The fire of the Spirit of God is necessary in the body of Christ to burn away the schisms that naturally occur because we live and operate in a cursed environment. The spiritual fire enables us to transcend the influence of a sinful world so that there is agreement within the body. God ignited this spiritual fire at Pentecost, and He expects us to keep it burning on the altar of our hearts so that the church can overcome the world. This spiritual fire is calling Pentecostals, Baptists, Methodists, Presbyterians, Episcopalians, Catholics, non-denominationalists, and all others under the Christian banner to unite in action to transform the environment in which we live.

Unit 2

Understanding Demonic Influence

Spiritual Principle: The letter kills but the Spirit gives life.

Chapter 4

Subject to Supernatural Influence

Godly Influence

We know that God created humans in His image and designed us to abide in His presence while using divinely given gifts to do His will. In our struggles to understand God's creative purpose for humanity, the Spirit and the Word help us to realize we were designed to be influenced by God. In order for humanity to believe, trust, worship, and love God, we must understand the strong influence He has on our lives. God influences our lives by providing all that is needed to fulfill our purpose of existence. The Word of God informs us that we exist because God shared of Himself what was needed to give life to humanity. God created humanity in a manner that allows Him to occupy the empty spaces in our existence. This occupation allows us to share existence, life, and purpose with God.

Because we share so much with God we become subject to the things of God. The more we share with God the more His presence and nature influence our existence, lives, and purpose. We begin to realize that we exist for His pleasure and are given life to fulfill His purpose. We also understand that God's pleasure and purpose are not driven by selfish motives of grandeur. God's pleasure involves sharing all of what He is and all that He has with us according to His will and love for creation. Because God created in love, all things were designed to operate for the good of the whole. Nothing was created to take without giving what is needed for other aspects of creation. This process could be called the creation cycle of existence.

The creation cycle of existence is demonstrated in the ecological relationship between animals, humans, and plants. Plants generate and release oxygen, which is needed in the breathing process of animals and humans. Animals and humans receive the oxygen generated by plants and give off carbon dioxide as a byproduct of their breathing process. Plants, on the other hand, use carbon dioxide as a part of photosynthesis, their food-making process. Therefore, humans, animals, and plants all benefit in this giving and receiving process. Our design to be used by God was given in order for God to share of Himself with all creation so that the blessedness of His existence can be experienced by all.

While we know that God requires much of us, we also understand that God gives far more than He asks. God occupies our emptiness in love so that we have no want. This relationship between God and humanity is illustrated in Psalm 23. This psalm indicates how God guides, provides, protects, and comforts humanity on our journey into eternal life. God's love is also confirmed in the first chapter of the Gospel of John; God indicated His love for creation with the ultimate sacrifice of leaving the glories of heaven to become a man and die for the salvation of creation.

God designed all creation to be an extension of His presence so that He could interact with any part of creation through what He made. God often inhabits the natural things in creation to instruct and direct the spiritual things of creation. Yes, He uses bushes, animals, water, fish, and rocks to intervene in the lives of humans as He leads us to eternity. God even uses spiritual beings of His creation (angels) to intervene into the lives of humans. The angels were designed as supernatural (spiritual) beings with the ability to influence the lives of humans according to the will of God. There seem to be three main reasons for angels being able to influence the lives of humans.

Reason #1: To serve as guardians or ministering spirits to the children of God.

God created angels to have charge over the lives of humans (Psalm 91:11). Angels are ministering spirits sent by God to minister to those who will inherit salvation (Hebrews 1:14). This scripture indicates that angels are designed to serve God by assisting in the well-being of humanity. Biblical accounts indicate angels are given charge over humanity according to the will of God. This charge implies both limited responsibility and authority over the actions of humanity. This limited authority is not designed (nor can it) to override the freewill of humanity given by God. This God-given influence over the lives of humans puts angels in the position of being responsible for protection and guidance of humans according to the will of God. Thus we have developed the concept of guardian or ministering angels.

Guardian angels are instructed to interact with the lives of humans during times of danger, discomfort, and division. The ministering angel concept is illustrated in the life of Jesus after the devil left Him in the wilderness and when He was struggling to accept His purpose in Gethsemane. A guardian or ministering angel awakened Peter and led him out of prison. Guardian angels are also mentioned in the Old Testament such as when Abraham and Lot were visited before the destruction of Sodom and Gomorrah. Both Isaiah and Daniel received visits by angels during significant incidents in their lives. In all these incidents, the angels played a major role in helping people understand and fulfill God's purpose for their lives.

The Bible illustrates that angels who intervened into the lives of humanity clearly informed those they were sent to serve not to worship them. The angels referred to themselves as fellow servants for the children of God and for those who have the testimony of Jesus. They understood and conveyed to others that only God is to be worshiped. They also conveyed that they were servants of God charged with aiding humans according to His will (Revelation 19:10). Biblical accounts indicate that angels did not intervene in every situation in the lives of the people mentioned. They seemed to intervene when the situation had eternal implications in the lives of

individuals, or the kingdom of God. They also intervened in important matters that demonstrated the sovereignty or glory of God.

Reason #2: To send messages into the lives of God's children.

Angels are spiritual beings designed to abide in the presence
and experience the fullness of God. They are endowed with spiritual
abilities, not bound to the natural laws of the universe. They can take
natural form but are not limited to the restraints of the flesh even
when they are in human form. Thus, they are referred to as being
supernatural in abilities and appearance.

Angels were created with supernatural abilities so that they
could serve the will of God in all situations. In biblical accounts
angels help humans to overcome situations beyond their natural
abilities such as when the angel gave water to Hagar and Ishmael in
the wilderness, tamed the lions for Daniel, or led Peter out of jail.
The angels possess abilities that are superior to those of humans,
who are restricted to the natural laws of the universe. These abilities
allow them to travel to places in an instant and operate natural forces
of the earth according to the will of God.

With their supernatural abilities the angels are able to take on the
form and presence of people according to the will of God. With this
ability God can use angels to send messages into the lives of people
during distressful times. In ministering I have heard many accounts
of people being visited by deceased loved ones during difficult times
in their lives with messages of instruction and encouragement. The
persons in the visitation are described as looking, acting, and even
reacting in the personality of the deceased loved ones. Since we
know that our loved ones are asleep and resting from their labors
in the Lord, we realize that God is sending messages through the
angels.

God sees us in our distress and uses the supernatural abilities
of His angels to talk to us in a form that comforts us. God knows
all about those individuals who are dear to our hearts, and He cares
enough about us to send messages that are in their hearts as they
leave this world. There are many accounts of visitations of loved
ones to people who are grieving to let them know they are all right.
In other accounts God has sent strangers into the lives of people who

are in need of help and comfort. These people seem to come out of nowhere and then just disappear.

The Bible has many accounts of angels showing up in the form of people like the two angels who led Lot and his family out of the destruction of Sodom and Gomorrah. The Bible also instructs us to be careful how we treat strangers because some of us have entertained angels without being aware of it. Whether in the personalities of our loved ones or strangers that we meet, God uses the supernatural abilities of His angels to send messages into the lives of His children. In His wisdom God is able and knows when these special messages of love are needed in our lives.

Reason #3: Because humans are subject to the influence not only of holy angels but also of unholy angels.

Humans are subject to supernatural influences because we were designed to be subject to the influence of God. However, because of Adam and Eve's disobedience we are also subject to demonic supernatural influences. Through original sin that is inherited from our first parents and actual sin which we commit ourselves, we are subject to the forces of evil that work against the will of God. Sin caused humanity to enter a state of being cursed and experiencing torment. Even before God spoke the nature of the curse, Adam and Eve had already experienced shame, fear, and torment (Genesis 3:6-10).

The actions of Adam and Eve set humanity on a course of suffering and inheritance of a cursed nature that is both subject to and drawn to sin (Genesis 6:5-6; John 3:19). The demonic forces that influence humanity are spiritual and operate against the will of God. They are supernatural beings created by God that choose to defy and reject the will and sovereignty of God. These beings as indicated in Ephesians 6:12 come from heavenly places because they are fallen angels that joined under the influence of Satan in the heavenly rebellion. Any being that rejects and works against the purpose of God becomes demonic in nature and unholy. Therefore, these angels became demons and involve themselves in unholy acts that work against God's purpose for creation.

The cursed and sinful nature of human flesh allows the unholy angels to influence humanity outside the will of God. These angels use their God-given abilities against the will of God much like humans may choose to use their God-given abilities contrary to the will and purpose of God. These angels (demonic forces) do not have authority over humanity and can't make us disobey God. Rather, they prompt us to be disobedient and rebellious through the tendencies and desires of our flesh. The unholy angels influence humanity to satisfy the flesh and its desires, which have negative results on human spiritual and emotional reactions. In our sinful situation we experience similar reactions as Adam and Eve when they were hiding in shame and afraid of the presence of God. Their sin, which was influenced by the devil through the serpent, caused them to fear the very presence they were created to be within (Revelation 12:7-9). The influence of these creatures causes us to reject our created purpose and exposes us to purposes contrary to the will of God.

Fallen Angels

It is important to understand that demonic creatures are compulsive and obsessive in nature, and their influence has the same effect on humanity. Much of the compulsive and obsessive behaviors we see are a result of the influence of these forces. The fallen angels are compulsive in nature and cannot be satisfied because they have already rejected all that there is. Created in heaven, they experienced the fullness of God but were not satisfied. There is nothing beyond the fullness of God to satisfy them. This concept of no repentance is illustrated in Hebrews 6:4-8 because the angels have already experienced the powers of the age to come and the fullness of God. Therefore, they remain in an eternal state of unfulfillment and non-satisfaction.

The angels who rebelled against God were influenced by Satan, who is believed to have been the covering cherub illustrated in Ezekiel 28:11-19. Some scholars believe this description of the fall of Lucifer, the covering cherub, is used in Isaiah 14:12-21 and Ezekiel 28:11-19 to illustrate the offenses and fall of the kings of Babylon and Tyre. While this concept is debated among scholars, the book of Revelation clearly illustrates the influence of Satan on the angels who rebelled against God. Part of Satan's motive was to be God himself, and he led one-third of the angels to believe they could be their own god and worshiped by others. This rebellion caused the unholy angels to be cast out of heaven into eternal darkness and damnation (Revelation 12:7-9; Isaiah 14:12-15). Because they were not satisfied among the stars, the Almighty cast them down into pits and utter darkness.

By rebelling against God the unholy angels caused themselves to be locked into an existence of non-satisfaction and forever wanting more. These unholy principalities of power seek hosts that they can influence and occupy (Matthew 12:43-45). They attempt to fill the emptiness that exists in humans who are not filled with the Spirit of God. Sin causes humans to shun the presence of God and become subject to other forces. If we are not occupied by the presence of God, then we will become occupied by something else.

Unholy spirits are able to influence humans to satisfy the desires of their flesh due to the cursed nature that desires what is contrary to God. Because of their compulsive nature, demons escalate the natural desires and compulsions of humans. This escalation of desires often leads to addictions and obsessions that destroy relationships, fulfillment, and lives. Spirits of addictions and obsessions cannot be satisfied and often lead humans who are caught up in them to hurt themselves and others. These types of demonic obsessions have been experienced through serial killers, stalkers, rapists, and drug addicts. Many of them speak of uncontrollable urges and even voices that push them to cause destruction and death. Demonic addictions are experienced through drug addicts and the never-ending urges of superstars. Society has witnessed the insatiable urges of superstars such as Marilyn Monroe, Elvis, Anna Nicole Smith, and Michael Jackson. Each one of these superstars experienced overwhelming urges and desires that ultimately led to their untimely deaths.

Chapter 5

The Struggle Against Principalities and Powers

Self-Transformation

The devil can transform himself into an angel of light (2 Corinthians 11:12-15). This nature of self-transformation is Satan's greatest offer of deception. The holy angels are transformed according to the will of God. Therefore, their spiritual abilities work to fulfill the purpose and will of God. Demonic influence offers humanity self-transformation and satisfaction of the flesh. This type of influence leads humanity away from the purpose and will of God. The desire for self-transformation led humanity into self-will and desire. This type of desire can lead to self-worship rather than God-worship. The first humans' attempt to redefine themselves apart from God caused them to be separated from God. Because God designed humanity with purpose, any attempts to redefine ourselves outside the will of God cause us to cease operating in divine purpose.

The devil offered humanity self-transformation in the Garden of Eden, and Adam and Eve accepted on our behalf. This act of rebellion was accomplished not by overpowering humanity but rather through deception and enticing Eve to satisfy the lust of the eye, the lust of the flesh, and the pride of life as found in Genesis 3:6 and 1 John 2:16. The demonic influence of Satan came through human (carnal) reasoning and fleshly desires. It was encouraged through a failure to speak truth to situations and a willingness to go along to fit in. Since Adam was not deceived, his sin involved his failure to speak God's truth to the serpent and Eve, and his willingness to follow Eve contrary to God's will. As a result, they ended up not being with God and not satisfied but rather in sin and torment.

The demonic influence Adam and Eve experienced in the garden has played a major role throughout the history of humanity in failed relationships, troubled business relationships, slavery systems, and wars. The sickness of sin released by Adam and Eve has infiltrated every aspect of human existence whether instituted by man or God. This sickness is even present in the church that Christ gave Himself to save. Even now in a church that is more than two thousand years old, the same temptations of the first humans taint the freewill process of humanity. The enemy seems to take pleasure in using the fleshly flaws of humanity to put the church to shame.

Human Reasoning vs. Spiritual Intuition

One could ask the question, "Why are demonic influences so prevalent in the church today?" Churches and ministries seem to be at an all-time high in prosperity and visibility, yet our societies around the world are increasingly chaotic and destructive. More and more church organizations are experiencing scandals that are covered up by the church and allowed to continue. Could the church be suffering from the effects of self-transformation achieved through humanistic thinking and demonic influence?

In a time in history in which we have the written instructions of God for the church and the Holy Spirit active in the lives of humanity, it would seem that the church would be more of a transforming voice in the world. Where was the voice of the church in Germany while Hitler's regime was planning the genocide of the Jews? Where was the voice of the church in America when the country was being built with slave labor? One can even ask where the voice of the church is today while our country invades other nations under false pretenses. The silence of the church seems to indicate that we are rationalizing the actions of the world through a humanistic thought process.

Could the existing conditions of the church be the result of what the early church struggled with when the Judean Christians resisted the influence of Hellenization? Could they have seen the influence of Hellenistic thinking leading the church on a path of humanistic reasoning that could hinder it from being Spirit-led? The concept of Hellenism revolved around the reasoning or rational thought of humanity. Is this not the same concept the serpent offered to humanity in the garden? Adam and Eve's ability to reason for themselves independent of God's guidance led to their downfall (Genesis 3:1-7). Could it be that this path has led society and the church to a place where we depend more on our ability to reason than on seeking God's guidance and intervention in our lives?

The ministry and teachings of Jesus focused on reestablishing relationships between God and humanity. Jesus illustrated His submission to His Father's will in His life, teaching, and interactions with others. Jesus taught His disciples to depend on God's guidance and intervention in the affairs of the church and their personal lives. He also indicated that the disciples would be orphans without it (John 14:15-21). Jesus promised them the intervention of the Holy Spirit and breathed on them as He spoke before sending them out. Here Jesus illustrates the speaking spirit that brings things into being (John 20:21-22).

In the book of Acts, the disciples waited in Jerusalem for the power of the Holy Spirit as Jesus had instructed them so they could become His witnesses to the world (Acts 1:4-8). The disciples followed these instructions as they shared in the upper room Pentecost experience. For the most part, throughout the Gospels the disciples are depicted as witnesses and supporters of the miraculous acts of Jesus. However, after Pentecost they became the instruments God used to perform miraculous acts of separation from sin, sickness, and death. Peter and John interacting with a lame man only had to speak a word and miraculous healing took place (Acts 3:1-19). All of the apostles performed miraculous signs and wonders (Acts 5:12-16) as well as Philip in Samaria (Acts 8:4-8).

The early Christians struggled mightily against the influence of Hellenistic thinking that had become prevalent in many of the cultures of their day. The Judean Christians rejected the practices that led to humanistic, reasoning-oriented Christianity. The strong expression of this type of religious thought seemed to move the church away from seeking spiritual guidance to becoming more dependent on natural reasoning. One could argue that this type of thinking leads to a more secular-oriented Christian practice and makes Christians more subject to demonic influences.

While rational reasoning has produced some important break-throughs in society and in the Christian church, we must ask our-selves: have we replaced seeking God's spiritual guidance with the reasoning of humanity? Are we reasoning our way through ministry and calling it God's will? Have we come to the point where we believe we know the mind of God? This seems to be the type of independent and humanistic thinking the serpent offered Eve in the garden, and it separated humanity from God.

The early disciples spent time seeking God's instruction through the Holy Spirit about matters concerning living for God and doing the work of ministry. The book of Acts is full of illustrations of the early disciples being instructed by the Holy Spirit and angels about the work of ministry such as with Philip on the way to Gaza (Acts 8:26-40); Peter's interaction with Cornelius (Acts 10:1-48); and Barnabas and Saul's assignment at Antioch (Acts 13:1-12). The early disciples invited the Spirit of God into the management of church affairs through fasting and praying in unity.

Could it be that our dependency on our own reasoning has led us down a path that causes us to invite God into our affairs only at cer-tain opportune times? Are we acting on our rational thinking before we take the time to consult God? The Bible teaches us that Jesus stands at the door and knocks, but He waits for our acknowledg-ment and invitation to come in (Revelation 3:20). Could the church have Jesus standing at the door waiting to be invited into our affairs? While we reason in our board meetings and rationalize our plans, do we take time to invite Jesus in and listen to His advice? Could the constant trouble the church faces with church leaders getting caught up in scandals and ministries experiencing difficult situations be the result of our lack of seeking God? Could God be allowing these incidents so that He can get our attention? Have our reasoning pro-cesses become so loud that we cannot hear Jesus knocking?

Humanistic reasoning has led us to believe the spiritual gifts of the early church such as prophecy and discerning of spirits have ceased. However, these gifts began to operate in the masses only after the outpouring of the Holy Spirit at Pentecost (Acts 2:1-4). Could it be because we do not expect God to intervene, or because we simply don't take time to consult Him in our affairs? We must remember that our rational thought processes are limited and subject to demonic influences while the wisdom of God is infinite and incorruptible. We must follow the example of Jesus, who sought the wisdom of the Father while He was a man to fulfill His purpose on the earth. If Jesus needed to seek His Father's guidance, how much more do we need to depend on God's guidance and influence in our lives?

If we are to overcome the influence of demonic forces in our personal lives and church affairs, we must take time to seek the presence of God, the wisdom of God, and the intervention of God. It is important that we first acknowledge that we are not sufficient in our own selves. For the Bible teaches us that in our weaknesses we are made strong (2 Corinthians 12:9-10). We must spend time in the Spirit of God, through prayer and meditation, so that He can change the conditions in our lives that unlock the blessings He already wants to give us.

One hundred years ago the Spirit of God moved within the church calling believers to a higher spiritual commitment. The focus of this movement revolved around what is known as the Azusa Street experience. The Azusa Street experience ushered in a movement that was designed to lead the Christian church back to dependence on spiritual intuition rather than human reasoning. This experience is attributed as the beginning of the Pentecostal denomination in America.

Those who were searching for a deeper and more committed spirituality than provided by the traditional Catholic and Protestant churches were drawn to this movement. Many of those who sought spiritual fulfillment based solely on the Word gravitated to more traditional denominations. This time of spiritual transition has produced some interesting divisions and movements within Protestant churches over the past century. As a result, many non-denominational churches today attempt to bring a balance between traditionalism and non-traditionalism in the worship experience.

During this same time period traditional denominations have also experienced movements that seek a balance between Spirit-led and Word-based worship and lifestyle practices. One such movement known as the full-gospel movement incorporated Word-based experiences with spiritual fervor and influence in worship and daily living. Could it be that the Pentecostal movement was not an end in itself but rather a transitional phase God was using to create the proper balance between seeking spiritual intuition and using human reasoning to guide our worship and Christian living?

Spiritual movements such as Azusa Street and the full-gospel movement are not designed to create denominations but to empower the body of Christ to separate from the cursed things and move into the presence of God. The body of Christ must not be so individualistically focused that we neglect the gifts and revelations shared with other parts of the body. The acceptance of these gifts and revelations and their assimilation into the framework of our congregations is God's opportunity to empower us to overcome the things that hinder the church.

If the church shifts to being guided totally by human reasoning in our worship experiences, then we will only experience zeal according to knowledge in our worship but deny the power thereof. This occurs when the church depends upon human knowledge and intellect to guide its actions, which systematically leads to shutting God out of the decision-making process. We begin to rationalize what was really meant when the Scriptures were written. We ponder which ones are good for our knowledge and understanding. This approach becomes problematic when we rationalize that some passages of Scripture were only relevant for certain periods of time while others can be discounted. This type of rationalization leads us to supplant the wisdom of God's Word with our own human reasoning. We must be aware that human reasoning is a powerful tool given by God to humanity, but it is not designed to operate independently of God. When we attempt to reason without God's influence, we deny His authority over our existence and His power to lead us through life experiences.

If the church shifts totally to spiritual intuition, then we experience a zeal of God but not according to knowledge. This occurs when we depend on being Spirit-led but neglect understanding the Word of God that leads us to spiritual oneness with God. We must keep in mind that not every spirit is of God. It is possible to have spiritual experiences outside of the will of God. After all, the devil is a spirit and is often involved in spiritual experiences of humanity that are not in accord with the Word of God.

The Word of God teaches us that to worship Him, we must do so in Spirit and according to His Word (John 4:23-24). The words of instruction and inspiration from the Lord are designed to lead us in our spiritual experiences with God. Without understanding of the Word, we will find ourselves subject to spiritual and emotional experiences that are contrary to God's will. Lack of understanding makes it easier for us to get caught up in the emotions and inspiration of people and be contrary to the will of God. When this happens, we cannot hear from God and walk in a false understanding of God's will while feeling that we are doing the right thing.

A good understanding of biblical teaching helps us to realize what spirits are of God. We must try the spirits by the Word of God for God's Spirit bears witness of His Word. The Spirit of the Lord works in agreement with the Word of God in ushering us into the presence of God. Our worship must be in His presence, and we must be in agreement with His Word and His Spirit. Even though the three persons of the Trinity are responsible for different attributes of God, they are always in agreement and operate in oneness. The church must learn to operate in oneness with God and with one another.

Understanding the Nature of the Enemy

In our struggles with demonic influence we as believers must understand that devils originated in heaven rather than in hell. They were created in the presence of God and experienced the fullness of His glory. Therefore they are aware of where we are trying to go and what is needed to get there. Demonic forces understand that fulfillment of purpose involves maintaining the proper relationship with God and each other. They know what will hinder those relationships and are willing to encourage and assist us in activities that disrupt our relationships. They also have knowledge of our divine purpose and are able to entice us to operate contrary to that purpose.

The unholy angels, including Satan, are supernatural beings but they do not have authority in the earthly realm. God gave that authority to humanity to fulfill His purposes in creation. Unholy angels, demons, or devils cannot bring sin and death into the realm of humanity. Therefore, they use deception to cause us to bring sin and death into our own lives and the lives of our brothers and sisters. They are able to play with our earthly desires and emotions in attempts to separate us for God. They understand that in separating us from God our natural proclivities would cause us to operate outside of the will of God.

As God informed Cain, sin is a pervasive spirit that desires to rule over us, but we can rule over it. Jesus told Peter that Satan desired to sift him as wheat, but He had prayed that Peter's faith would not fail. These scriptures inform us that we were designed by God to overcome the influence of demonic forces and that Jesus has empowered us to overcome the temptations of evil. Both Cain and Peter were attacked by forces of evil to separate them from God and to fill their hearts with emotions and desires contrary to the will of God. God intervened in both of their situations before the enemies of creation could cause them to act against the will of God. However, Cain 's situation turned out to be more destructive than Peter's, because he did not accept God's intervention.

Guarding Your Heart

As followers of Jesus Christ we must be careful of our thoughts. The Bible informs us that a man becomes what he thinks in his heart. Therefore demonic forces wait for our thoughts to betray us. Due to our human experience, sometimes our thoughts reveal desires that are contrary to God's Word and will. Such thoughts are manifested through fleshly appetites. These thoughts originate in our mind, and demonic forces begin working to cause us to receive them in our hearts. The enemies of creation have access to our minds, but our hearts belong to God.

We often find ourselves struggling with thoughts that are contrary to God's Word and our purpose. Such thoughts can be generated by a touch, a word, a sweet fragrance, or a pretty sight. Oftentimes we give up when such thoughts become lust and we think we want to go along with sinful activities because our bodies respond. We must remember that we are spiritual beings in fleshly bodies. Our bodies will react to fleshly stimulation even when we do not want to engage in sinful acts in our hearts. We have to learn that we are not our flesh and to tell the flesh no by the power of God.

Thoughts of the flesh can drive us to lust such as when David saw Bathsheba bathing from his rooftop. He allowed the thoughts of his mind to enter into his heart, and it became lust that prevented him from acting like a righteous king. David did not hear with his heart when his servant said "Isn't this Uriah's wife?" and his lust drove him to acts of adultery, deception, and murder. David's lust and deception blinded him to Uriah's loyalty to God's law, Jewish tradition, and the king. It was only when Nathan informed David that he was the man of sin that he fully realized the weight of his actions. When lust enters into our hearts it blinds us to the will and purpose of God for our lives, and our natural senses take over to our demise.

The concept of lust can also be tied to feelings of pride and self-exaltation. Herod's experience with the people of Tyre and Sidon demonstrates the destructive effects of prideful lusts. Herod allowed the people to claim that he spoke with the voice of a god and not a man. Herod's pride prevented him from giving God glory and honor, and God killed him.

We must train ourselves to keep thoughts that are contrary to God's will and purpose from entering our heart. We often attempt to fight such lust with our mental capacities and fail. Our mental capacities are carnal and subject to demonic influence. We should be aware that this type of battle comes to all of us in different forms. We must prepare for such battles before they are upon us. We prepare by allowing our hearts to be filled with God's Word, Spirit, and love. With our hearts filled with the presence and power of God, there is no room for lustful, fearful, hateful, and prideful thoughts. The power of God in our hearts also enables us to overcome the forces we struggle with in our minds. By engaging the power of God we transfer the battlefield from the mental realm to the spiritual realm. On the spiritual battlefield we have the power of God to aid in our struggle.

Because demonic forces originated in heaven, we must keep in mind that they are supernatural beings and subject to the power of God. They attempt to deceive us into engaging them in battle with natural and hellish methods such as anger, doubt, and pride. The Bible gives examples of dealing with demonic forces, such as when Michael disputed with Satan concerning the body of Moses. Michael did not use slanderous accusations against Satan. Michael, who is a supernatural being himself, used the authority of God the rebuke the devil (Jude 9). Jesus was also confronted by the devil in the wilderness, and He used the Word and authority of God to rebuke Satan. These illustrations inform us that these battles are not for us to fight alone, but we must engage the presence and power of God to overcome these evil influences.

Demons are rebelling against God and only use us as pawns in their attempts to disrupt God's plan and prevent us from fulfilling divine purpose. Knowing that God is aiding us in our struggles against demonic forces, we can prepare ourselves to resist evil. This resistance involves denying our flesh the things that are contrary to the will of God and separate us from His presence. God has given us instruments of righteousness to assist us in our struggles. These instruments of righteousness are designed to usher and keep us in the presence and power of God.

Instruments of Righteousness

Fasting and praying are two powerful instruments God has given humanity to avoid the influence of demonic forces. Fasting involves denying ourselves food while abstaining from some of the other pleasures of the flesh. Eating, drinking, and sex are three of the strongest natural drives of human nature. In fasting, believers deny themselves the pleasures of these drives. Through fasting believers learn to deny these pleasures and build spiritual discipline. Because unholy spirits are compulsive and excessive in nature, they like to be fed. The more believers deny themselves, the less influence unholy forces have on their lives.

By self-denial, believers make themselves less suitable for ungodly spirits and take on the nature of Christ. In His life on earth Christ demonstrated the practice of self-denial for the fulfillment of

His Father's will. Fasting helps us to take on the nature of Christ and prepare our being for the presence of God. God occupies creation that is obedient to His will and avoids evil. Our self-denial allows God to become more active in our lives and draws us closer to His presence. Through fasting, our spiritual being gains power over the human vessel God has given us to exist in. The Holy Spirit empowers us to overcome the influence that demonic forces exert on our natural being and prepares us to be in God's presence and operate in His will.

Prayer is another important instrument of righteousness in our struggles against demonic forces. Prayer involves two-way communication with God that creates spiritual intimacy in our relationship with God. Spiritual intimacy involves the giving of ourselves to God and conditions us for abiding in His presence. Prayer helps us to understand that we belong to God and that He provides for what belongs to Him. In prayer we are able to share our desires with God, and He is able to instruct us as to how our desires fit or do not fit into His plan for our lives. He is also able to inform us how to position ourselves to avoid hindrances to our purpose.

Through prayer we are able to reach God so that He can share with us and take away our want. Because God is the ultimate provider of creation, being in His presence removes want from our lives because our spirit realizes that whatever is needed exists in God. Demonic forces use our sense of want to entice us to operate contrary to the will of God. The sense of want implies that something has not been provided for us. With the absence of want we become less suitable for the presence of demonic forces and more suitable for the Spirit of God. Because God removes our want, we become free to operate in the things God planned for our lives. Prayer helps us to understand that our needs and righteous desires are being provided for as we operate in the will of God.

The Word informs us not to be anxious for anything but to present our requests to God with prayer and supplications with thanksgiving (Philippians 4:6). We must be able to be thankful and enjoy the journey of moving into our blessings even before we receive them. My wife and I are experiencing this type of journey as we write this book. I have been working full-time in ministry for the past eight years, and God instructed my wife to leave her job and work with me in ministry two years ago. God provided resources in the ministry where we were serving that enabled my wife to receive a salary. One year ago God reassigned us, and the ministry we are currently serving does not have the resources for a paid position for my wife, but her skills are needed there.

My wife and I are paying our obligations with one salary, and both of our children are preparing for their futures and require our financial assistance. I got anxious about being able to take care of our obligations and asked her about finding a temporary job. She became anxious about helping me. She applied for several positions and nothing happened. She applied for another job that she was highly qualified to do well. She got the job and something happened with the company that caused to job to fold up within two months. She applied for another job working in a Christian environment that she was highly qualified for but did not get the job.

Through prayer my wife and I have been able to reevaluate our situation and decided to enjoy the journey we are on, knowing that God knows where we are. We are not addled but busy working to build the ministry He has appointed us to. We have begun to focus on the blessedness of how God has provided in the past year and allowed us to touch the lives of so many people. The Holy Spirit reminded us that God knows where we are, and He has provided for all our needs and then some. We realize that God is giving us a new testimony to share with His children about abiding in the purpose of God, and we are thankful. We are thankful for being in the situation God has placed us in and have learned to enjoy the wonderful journey that we are on. Through our relationship of prayer with God, the Holy Spirit also empowers us to overcome the natural proclivities that make us subject to demonic forces.

Chapter 6

Overcoming Demonic Influence

3-D Love

The demonic influence of evil has led to many destructive addictions and obsessions in society. However, it is important to understand that humanity does not have to yield to the influences of evil. Our redemption is secured by Jesus Christ's death and resurrection and can be maintained through the power of the Holy Spirit. There is a concept I refer to as "3-D love" in the kingdom of God that is essential to overcoming demonic influence: the love of God, love of self, and love of others, all of which keep us balanced in our relationships. We first have to love God in order to love ourselves and others. Our relationship with God empowers us to obey Him and avoid cursed things that hinder our relationship with Him. As humans we cherish and are drawn to what we love. Therefore, our love for God helps us to stay in relationship and be near Him.

Regarding love of self, it is important to understand the difference between loving oneself and being in love with oneself. When we are in love with ourselves, we will do what pleases us even if it is harmful to us. This is where demonic influences are deadly to us. Their influence leads us to satisfy ourselves to our own personal harm and the harm of those around us. However, when we love ourselves we will deny ourselves for the good of ourselves. Our love for God and ourselves moves us beyond the self-infractions and indulgences that are necessary for self-denial. This was the type of love Jesus expressed when He was in the garden. Being in love with ourselves is based on things that please us, but love itself is the undying nature of God that bonds us to someone or something, even when they are not with us or pleasing us.

This same concept applies to loving others rather than just being in love with others. If we truly love someone, we will not hurt them or help them to hurt themselves. We will deny them from pleasing themselves for their own good. If we love them as we love ourselves, then we will not treat them in a way that is against the will of God. Such love empowers us to understand others even when they are not acting like children of God. We are able to overcome the human frailties that cause separation and hatred between us. Jesus demonstrated this type of love on the cross when He asked God to forgive those who did not know what they were doing.

God has made us His children and given us the gift of the Holy Spirit to fill our existence and empower us against demonic influences. As children of God we must be subject to the presence and authority of the Holy Spirit. When we do this, we eliminate the space and opportunity for demonic influences. The Holy Spirit puts the sinful nature of our flesh in subjection and enables us to overcome desires of the flesh. It is difficult for us to hear the siren call of desires when we are listening to God. It is difficult to run to them when we are wrapped up in God's Spirit.

Adoption of the Children of God

Because God gave dominion of the earth to humanity (Genesis 1:26), creation has been waiting for us to take our rightful place as the covering beings of creation. Creation has been waiting for the adoption of God's children and the redemption of the spiritual body. The adoption occurred when Christ gave back to us our birthright at Calvary. In this adoption we were united again with the family of our heavenly Father and became the children of God (Romans 8:14-17; Galatians 4:1-7; 1 Peter 1:3-25).

The redemption of the spiritual body will occur in the resurrection (1 Corinthians 15:52-58; Revelation 20:4-6; Luke 20:36), and humanity shall regain the spiritual image of the Father (1 Corinthians

15:49; 1 John 3:1-4). In the redemption of the body, we shall become like God (not by self-transformation but through the power of God). Only God can lead us and take us to what He has prepared for us. When God transforms us to be like Him, we will be able to speak the things of God so that creation will not have to suffer the curse of humanity (Genesis 3:17). If we are no longer suffering through the curse then creation is free from the curse. The lion is waiting on the redemption of the body so that he can lie down with the calf, and the adder is waiting so that he can play with the little child (Isaiah 11:6-9). They have been suffering through our guilt and bearing the violence of our curse.

We are currently living between the adoption into the family of God and the redemption of the spiritual body. We are joint-heirs with Christ, and our inheritance is reserved in heaven. Therefore, we are expected to walk in the hope of that inheritance. In our walk we are expected to be holy in our imitation of a holy God (1 Peter 1:14-19). Our holy walk of life can be accomplished only through the Holy Spirit, who empowers us to mortify (separate) ourselves from the deeds of the body (the cursed things). The Spirit leads us to be children of God and helps us in our progress toward the reality that God has for us when the revelation of humanity occurs at the appointed time, at the Chief Shepherd's appearance. As we walk in this hope, we become the glory of God within the world and provide a beacon of light for those who have not been adopted into the family of God.

Keys to the Kingdom

As children of God, we have been given the keys to the kingdom of heaven (Matthew 16:19). With these keys, we are expected to bind and release spiritual forces within this world. We have the promise that the power of God will operate within us as we carry out the will of God. God allows humanity to partner with Him in carrying out His will. Since the adoption, God has given us back some of the dominion we lost in Adam. This dominion over creation is given through our relationship with Christ Jesus. In this relationship, we are empowered to command the blessings of God. We are led by the Spirit as to what blessings to ask for and how to command such blessings.

As children of the kingdom of God we are expected to bind up the doors of cursing. These doors refer to the natural and spiritual influences of the flesh that lead to the cursed things which are outside the will of God for humanity in this world. We have the authority to bind temptation, hatred, division, sinful desires, sickness, and death that attack the flesh. By binding these forces we allow the Spirit within us to be free to operate in the will of God.

We are also given the authority to release the blessings of God into the lives of His people. The Spirit of God empowers and guides us to speak the spiritual blessings that exist within God from the spiritual world into the natural existence of humanity. These blessings are designed to benefit creation on earth. If the children of God do not speak the blessings of God then a void grows in the earth realm. Such a void is conducive to evil abiding and influencing humanity. It is like turning on lights in a room. When the lights are off there is a void of energy in the room, and darkness occurs where there is a void of energy. Darkness does not require energy to exist because it is the absence of light energy and it causes the absence of sight. Light, however, requires energy, and at the point of turning on the lights photonic energy instantly fills the void and the room is illuminated. The darkness cannot prevent the light from filling the void and illuminating the lives of those within the room (Genesis 1:3; John 1:4-5).

Similarly, evil is the absence of the presence of God and creates a spiritual void in which cursed things abide and influence. When the presence of God is activated then the void is filled with the essence of God, which brings life, holiness, righteousness, joy, peace, love, and all that is God. Just as darkness cannot prevent light from filling the void, evil cannot prevent righteousness from taking its place in our lives, nor can death prevent life from filling our existence, and hatred cannot prevent love from filling the void in our hearts. Evil is the absence of righteousness, death is the absence of life, hatred is the absence of love, and all of these demonic forces abide in the absence of the presence of God.

Creation is waiting and expecting the children of God to use the keys (God-given authority through Jesus Christ, Matthew 28:18) to bind the forces of evil that influence creation on earth and to lock the doors that lead us away from the presence of God. The body of Christ is also expected to label those doors that lead away from the presence of God and into darkness, disobedience, hatred, and death. This is why the church cannot be silent about the issues of life that are contrary to the Word of God. The church is expected to label the doors of cursing and blessing for the existing body of Christ and the next generation of children to be born again in Christ Jesus.

When the church is quiet on the issues of life a void is created in the earth realm and evil forces are allowed to influence humanity against the will of God. In darkness, we are ignorant of our surroundings and we make our way guessing, feeling, and sometimes stumbling over things because we do not know how to navigate properly. This is what occurs when the church fails to turn on the light of the Word of God to illuminate the issues of life. The church is expected to release the truth of God's Word that helps to guide humanity through the doors of blessing. Therefore, we must speak truth to powers and situations so that people are illuminated enough to discover the will of God for their lives.

Faith

First Corinthians 13:13 illustrates three of the keys to the kingdom that enable us to overcome demonic influences. The three keys are faith, hope, and love. Faith is a key that is both a gift and a fruit of the Spirit. This is the key that unlocks the possibilities of God into our lives. First the Spirit teaches us to trust God as our Father, Creator, and Sustainer. Then He teaches us to walk in the obedience of God's Word. When this gift activates in our lives it produces fruit that empowers us to speak the blessings of God. As we speak blessings our faith gives substance to the words that we speak because the Holy Spirit instructs us to speak the things that exist in God. Our faith provides assurance that these things exist in God even before we see them so that we will expect them. It is difficult for God to give us what we do not expect Him to do, unless it is a gift given to activate your faith in order to produce the fruit of faith (Hebrews 11:1)

Using the words of Neil Armstrong as he first walked on the moon, faith in God is the one small leap of a human that becomes a giant leap for humanity. Hebrews 11 reveals the faith hall of fame as evidence that trusting God allows one person to affect the lives of many. These testimonies instruct the body of Christ that through faith God has provided a better report for us in the promise of salvation. Our minds and spirits must be in agreement with the Word of God and the Spirit of God. Then with our hearts our trust in God allows us to speak the words of God and things begin to happen because we believe God's Word to the point that what we say happens.

The Bible teaches us that faith comes by hearing the Word of God (Romans 10:17). God's Word gives substance to what we believe about God and cancels the doubt and fear that come against our faith. The Word of God teaches us that creation has the ability to bring what is in God into natural and spiritual existence. The world and everything within it—trees, mountains, oceans, and creatures— were all in God, and through His living Word He spoke these things into natural existence. Because life is in the Word of God, we must be empowered by the Word to speak those things that are not **in this world** as if they already exist **in God.**

Hope

Hope refers to our expectation in God and unlocks our hearts to the promises of God. Our hope originates with the Word of God that reveals to us what God has promised us. As Romans 10:14 states, how can we believe in Him of whom we have not heard? Even our faith comes by hearing the Word of God, which reveals to us our rights in the kingdom of God. We have a right to trust God and expect Him to keep His promises. God has given us this right by binding Himself to His Word. Once we receive revelations of the promises of God, our faith allows those promises to become expectations (hope) in us.

Hope is also built on our desire for the things of God. We must delight ourselves in the promises of God. We do not expect the things of God like we wait for a hurricane to come on shore. We are delighted (willingly give ourselves) to the things that God has for us. Such delight causes an excitement in the body of Christ that binds the saints together and empowers us to operate in synergy. Remember, synergy is the ability to create more energy, power, or ability together than separately. It is this gift of hope that provides encouragement to the church and keeps the saints steadfast during difficult or prolonged times.

The gift of hope prevents the saints from slipping into grief, depression, and despair, which are different levels of the absence of hope. As we relinquish hope, we move closer to despair, or the absence of hope. Hope reminds us that God has not forsaken us even in our darkest hours and keeps us from giving up on life and God. Without hope we are lost to the void of despair. However, through hope we are united to the promises of God (Romans 8:17-21). Our minds are renewed by the Word of God and attuned to the Spirit's leading before responding to circumstances based on our own reasoning. This process generates hope as the Spirit of God speaks to our hearts and guides our actions based on His Word.

This gift of hope encourages and reminds us that we have the victory through our Lord and Savior Jesus Christ. This revelation brings about a spiritual excitement in the midst of our spiritual warfare with the things of the flesh. We begin to take pleasure through our hope in overcoming the cursed things and empowered to praise God for the journey back into His presence. We find hope in the promises of God that our spiritual labor will yield the fruits of righteousness and give us the victory over all things that are not of God (1 Corinthians 15:51-58).

Love

Love is the greatest key God has given to humanity, and it unlocks our motivation to be in the presence of God. Love is the very essence, nature, and motivating force of God. First John 4:7-8 teaches us that God is love and the things of God operate in love. Love is the greatest power, weapon, or ability we have. We are drawn to God through His love for us and our desire to return that love to Him. When two persons are in love, they are drawn together against all obstacles. Because God exists within all of us, we are drawn toward each other through the love of God. This is the force we must engage to enable humanity to overcome the hatred that has led to countless wars and conflicts.

Because we are separated from God, we separate from each other and learn to hate each other. When we reflect on biblical teachings we find that Cain did not have any legitimate reasons for hating his brother Abel. Yet he murdered him. Ignoring God's warning, Cain drew away from Him and allowed a void to occur that filled up with rage and hatred, and sin ruled over him. Hatred is the absence of love just as darkness is the absence of light; it occurs because of the absence of God's presence. Because God is life, where He is not present becomes a void in which hatred flourishes. When He abides in humanity, His nature also abides within us and that nature allows the attributes of God to flourish: goodness, mercy, longsuffering, understanding, temperance, peace, joy, and love.

Because God's act of creation was motivated by love, we are designed to love God and one another. Love of humanity is the motive behind all of God's actions even when it appears that He is working against us. Such an act occurred when He put humanity out of the garden to prevent humans from living forever in a sinful state. The most profound act of God's love toward fallen humanity occurred when He gave His only begotten Son to save all of creation (John 3:16). It is important that we emulate God in allowing our actions to be motivated by love. Love is what makes the difference between the missionary and the drug dealer who gives out shoes to children in the neighborhood.

Love begets love. Because God is love, His actions are motivated by His love, such as His desire to create beings like Himself. This is described in Genesis 1:26: "Then God said, Let us make man in our image, in our likeness, and let them rule over the fish of the seas and the birds of the air, over the livestock, over all the earth, and over all the creatures that move along the ground." Love abided within all of God's creation, and even the animals did not kill each other until after the fall of mankind. This is why the whole creation has been groaning for the adoption and revelation of the children of God. The creation desires to be back in harmony with God and with itself. It is love that will cause the lion to lie down with the lamb and the adder to play with the child.

While we await the revelation of the children of God, we must show love toward God and one another. Our show of love releases the nature of God within this cursed world, and that love begets love in others. The more we release our love the more the nature of love fills the void that already exists and the more God abides within this world. Only God can fill the void; His power and presence are only released through love (John 3:16). However, as children of God we must be prepared to overcome those who are not ready to receive our love because they have not embraced God enough to love Him in all His glorious forms. Sometimes we have difficulty recognizing, accepting, and embracing God when He does not look, act, and sound like we expect. Cain did not understand God's actions, and it resulted in his hatred being transferred to his brother.

We must remember that God was not created in our image; rather we were created in His image. The God of the entire universe is more complex than what we see in a mirror, hear with our ears, or conceive in our finite minds. God's love empowers us to embrace Him in whatever form He takes. If we do not use that love we cause a void to exist between us that allows evil emotions to grow and we enter into conflict with each other. God's love allows us to transcend the differences between us and find the common areas of humanity.

If we are to be the children of God, we must operate in the same power that our Father does. Love is the power that is able to fill the void within our hearts and prevents us from trying to fill it with worldly things that will not last. Love is the force God will use within all of creation to conquer death and eliminate evil. While we are waiting on the revelation of the children of God, it is important that we operate in the inspired words of the apostle Paul and let nothing separate us from the love of God that is in Christ Jesus our Lord (Romans 8:39).

Unit 3

Discovering Divine Purpose

**Spiritual Principle: You were created in the image
and likeness of God.**

Chapter 7

Seeing God

Isaiah's Experiences with God

The Old Testament prophet Isaiah gives a marvelous discourse concerning the discovery of divine purpose. It involves the discovery of divine purpose through seeing God, experiencing the heavenly witness, and getting real. Isaiah's thoughts, desires, and actions are changed by his experiences with God, the heavenly witnesses, and himself. He uses his personal testimony to illustrate this journey into divine purpose.

Isaiah's discourse begins with a loss in his life. In this case it was the death of King Uzziah. It is typical in biblical writing for authors to use the death or reign of kings as historical markers. However, things in biblical writing that seem coincidental often have significant spiritual implications. In his time of loss Isaiah experiences the Lord in multiple facets of life. One could draw the conclusion that the life of the king had somehow been a distraction in Isaiah's life. Isaiah indicates that the removal of the distractions associated with the king allowed him to see God. The story of Isaiah indicates that he moved from operating in the purpose of the king to discovering the purpose of God for his life. Often in our periods of loss and adjustments, we are able to experience what we have ignored. God gets our attention during periods of discomfort in ways that are difficult when we are in our comfort zone.

Whatever the reason, Isaiah experiences God as the authority of his life. In experiencing the sovereignty of God, we are able to begin putting life into proper perspective. We understand that God is above all things in existence and that all things are subject to Him. This realization shifts us from a self-centered concept of life to a God-centered reality that prevents things and people from clouding our vision of life. When we experience God in His rightful place of exaltation, the influence of other things diminishes in our lives. This is the beginning stage to understanding the concept of fearing God.

In fearing God, believers realize that God requires and deserves the ultimate respect of humans. We cannot exist without Him, and His ways and judgments are above our understanding. This is a very important step in releasing the natural hindrances to the discovery of divine purpose.

Isaiah experienced God's train filling the temple, which indicates the presence and influence of God filling the void of the vessel it occupied. It is important to experience God's power filling us — since we are now the temple of the Holy Spirit as Isaiah indicated. This discovery allows us to understand that God can, God desires, and God will fill the empty spaces in our lives. This power to fill is essential to our sense of fulfillment, which we seek through many earthly means. If we reflect on past experiences, we find that the desire for natural fulfillment often sent our lives into difficult and sinful situations. The trouble is that these situations start out tasting sweet to the flesh but leave our spirits even more empty and unfulfilled. To discover that God can fill those empty spaces is refreshing to our soul.

Experiencing the power of God to fill our lives helps us to stop focusing on our distractions in life and release the things that hinder us from fulfilling our purpose. This type of experience causes us to reflect on ourselves, our situations, and the realities around us. There is a profound line of self-reflection spoken by the scarecrow portrayed by Michael Jackson in the African-American version of *The Wizard of Oz* known as the Wiz. The scarecrow said that fame and fortune are all illusions and the only real thing is the relationship between two individuals. The untimely death of Michael Jackson left me wondering if he really understood or even listened to the words that came out of his own mouth when he said that line.

This scene in the movie occurs when Dorothy is about to leave the group and the Land of Oz. Reflections such as this should help us to look to a source that is higher, nobler, and more righteous than our natural sense of purpose.

The Flaming Sword

God shared a wonderful gift that will help usher humanity into the presence and purpose of God—and remain there. The gift I am referring to is what I call the Flaming Sword, or the agreement that exists between God's Word, Spirit, and love within the lives of believers. Through this agreement believers can activate the power of God to separate them from the cursed things in existence. The Flaming Sword that God gave to the cherubim in Genesis after Adam and Eve sinned was designed to keep the way to the tree of life. In much the same way the Flaming Sword activates in the lives of believers to keep them from the cursed things that would prevent them from abiding in the presence of God. The cursed things hinder us from seeing God in the multiple ways in which He intervenes in our lives. The Flaming Sword helps to separate us from those things that cloud or block our visions of God.

When believers operate in the divine nature the Flaming Sword operates fully in their lives to remove hindrances to the fulfillment of purpose as children of God. God shares of Himself with His children. Therefore we have access to the Flaming Sword, which is forged by the Word of God, ignited by the Spirit of God, and empowered by the love of God. The Word of God gives us the ability to know the things of God, which enables us to use the sword to separate the cursed things from the things of God. The Word gives substance to the sword to form a barrier between the things of God (eternal things) and the cursed things. God has placed creation power in His Word. Therefore, the sword is able to create barriers that are impassable to the cursed things. The Word of God is living and powerful enough to withstand the attacks of evil that believers face. Through the power of the Word the sword is able to separate evil spirits from the souls of humanity (Hebrews 4:12).

The Spirit of God gives the Flaming Sword the ability to help in times of weakness. The spiritual power of the sword is able to separate the cursed things from humanity's prayers so that the Spirit can send communications according to the will of God. The sword clears the way so that the Spirit can share revelations of the will of God within hearts and minds and help in weakness. When our outer man is weak the Holy Spirit intercedes on our behalf. The Spirit allows us to see God clearer as He interacts in our lives in different ways.

The Flaming Sword is ignited in the spirit person (souls) of those who are converted and have been baptized with the Holy Spirit. The power of the sword is not controlled by humanity; rather, the Spirit directs the power of the sword to interact in believers' lives, and it becomes more dominant during times of weakness. The sword is given to keep the way to the tree of life, and those who are saved through the blood of Jesus have received the promise of the tree of life (Revelation 22:2-3). The promise is made through the grace of our Lord and Savior Jesus Christ. Within the believer, the presence of God's Word, God's Spirit, and God's love acts in oneness (the Flaming Sword) to separate the things that bring curses to his or her life. The sword is the power of God's presence operating in the lives of believers to keep us from the worldly and evil influences that cause separation from God and loss of purpose.

Adam and Eve are the only human beings except Jesus who lived in the original nature of humanity. Everyone else was born into the cursed world with the sin nature that is separate from God. Humanity is far removed from the original nature and divine purpose; we are subject to the cursed nature. The influence of this sin nature was released as humanity spread across the world and developed society. The cursed nature became the learned nature and to some degree the nature that humanity strives to perfect. Jesus came to destroy the devil's power to enslave humanity through the sin nature (Hebrews 3:14-15) and became an atonement to free humanity from sin and reconcile us back to God.

In Revelation 2:7 the Spirit says to the church that they who overcome will be given the right to eat from the tree of life. As over-comers, humanity will no longer be cursed because of the sacrifice of Jesus Christ and will regain access to the tree of life. The Flaming Sword enables us to be overcomers of the things that bring curses and gives assurance of our right to the tree of life through Jesus Christ. God is removing the cursed things from His holy presence, but He has moved heaven and earth to keep us in His presence. If we separate ourselves from the cursed things, then we are able to remain in God's presence. If we hold onto the cursed things, then He will remove us from His presence along with the cursed things. The Flaming Sword allows us to keep the cursed things from our souls so that we remain in the presence of God and can walk in the fulfillment of purpose for our lives.

The Flaming Sword brings death to the former things that separated us from the presence of God. The sword brings death to our former sinful habits that prevent us from true worship of God—those things that hinder us from praying, distract us from reading God's Word, discourage us from entering the worship experience, and have taught us to disobey God. The sword operates with the personality of our soul person (spirit) to keep the cursed things from abiding within us, so that we can abide in the presence of God. As the sword comes to life within believers the cursed things die and the sword prevents them from resurrecting in our lives. The sin natures of humanity, whether inherent (original sin) or our own sin nature (actual sin), is forgiven and we are made alive unto God through the grace of our Lord and Savior Jesus Christ (Romans 5:8-21). As redeemed children of God we are able to truly worship Him. The Flaming Sword is given to God's children to keep the way of the tree of life that Jesus has established within us (Romans 5:21). The sword enables us to remain separated from the cursed things so that we can abide with God to fulfill our purpose in life.

It is important that we let go of the cursed things when the sword brings death to them. If we hold onto what God puts to death, we invite death to be a part of our existence. To invite death into our existence brings harm to us and to the body of Christ (Matthew 5:13). We must remember that God is removing the cursed things from His presence. If we let go of those things, then we can remain in the presence of God. If we hold onto them, then God will be forced to remove us along with the unholy things, even though He desires that we remain with Him. We must also remember that God is moving the cursed things into destruction, and to hold onto them would be to accept destruction. Humanity was not created for destruction but was created to be with God eternally in life and purpose.[1]

Spiritual Revelations

As we transcend our natural limitations, we can receive revelations of God. These revelations are designed to lead us into divine destiny (Revelation 4:1). The revelations are necessary for the fulfillment of our purpose in God. These revelations transform our spiritual awareness and awaken the Spirit of God that abides within us. The Spirit of God within us agrees with the revelations of God and empowers us to walk in those revelations. This spiritual empowerment includes instruction, encouragement, and revelations necessary to fulfill our destiny in God.

It is within what can be called a supernatural state of God's possibilities that we are able to speak the things that be not as though they are already. Because they exist in God, the Holy Spirit reveals them to us (1 Corinthians 2:9-10) and teaches us what to speak into our natural existence (Romans 8:26-27) according to the will of God.

In this supernatural state, we are able to be the light of the world that illuminates the nature of God operating in the lives of believers (Matthew 5:14-16). Through this illumination of the realm of humanity, God is glorified and humanity is elevated. We become imitators of God when we follow His revelations to remain separated from the cursed things and operate in His holiness and righteousness.

This supernatural power allows the world to see God in the midst of life that is granted to believers who remain separated from the cursed things. Through our ability to see God as sovereign in our lives, we are able to overcome those things that keep us from being in God's presence and cause us to lose purpose. In seeing God, we begin a spiritual journey in our natural existence that leads us into the fulfillment of divine purpose. Isaiah illustrated his experiences of seeing God like a rebirth of himself that produced a new creature capable of discovering his purpose in God.

Chapter 8

Experiencing the Heavenly Witness

Witness of the Angels

During Isaiah's discourse, he experiences heavenly witnesses in their reactions to the presence of God. The heavenly witnesses that he encountered were seraphim, angels that are known for abiding in the presence of God and giving Him honor and glory. Isaiah wrote of seeing, hearing, and being touched by the angels. He spoke of the angels acting in a unified manner which suggested the actions of one represented all of them. They were using their God-given abilities for the purpose that God gave them. Isaiah saw the seraphim using their gifts of wings in service that gave honor to God.

The seraphim used two of their three paired wings to cover their faces, indicating that their existence is not about self-glorification. The angels denied their own glory so that their existence would give glory to God. Self-glorification must be denied in the presence of God. The actions of the seraphim indicate that they exist to honor God with their lives and their gifts. They showed Isaiah how to use God-given gifts in a manner that reflects the purpose of their creation. Like Isaiah, it is important for us to realize that we exist and are given gifts for a greater purpose than our own glory.

The seraphim used another pair of wings to cover their feet, indicating that life was not about self-determination and that they were open to the will of God for their lives. This refusal to seek self-determination helps us to understand that we are not the masters of our destiny or the captains of our souls. This realization is paramount in our search for divine purpose. It is through this type of revelation that we are able to understand what God has for our lives. It is important to discover that we don't know our purpose and destiny in order to realize that we must seek it. *We often will not seek what we think we already have.*

Isaiah also saw the seraphim use the third pair of wings to fly, indicating that these gifts were given for the service of God. They were designed to fly in the presence and for the purpose of God. With self-glory and self-determination denied, the heavenly creatures demonstrated their service to God. This type of witness teaches us about denial of self-glorification and self-determination, which is a defense to the original satanic attack in the Garden. Humanity was deceived into seeking self-glorification and self-determination and lost their way. Through denial of our self and our desires, we are prepared to operate in the service of God. The desire for self-glorification and self-determination makes us vulnerable to the lust of the flesh, the lust of the eye, and the pride of life.

One of the seraphim cried to another "Holy, Holy, Holy is the Lord of hosts," giving honor to God in a triumphant manner. The angel indicated that the whole earth is full of His glory! The heavenly creatures used their gifts of speech to honor God and indicated His presence and involvement in the earth. This witness teaches us that God has designed creatures to be speaking spirits like Him. Speaking spirits are able to change the environment around them though the power of the spoken word given by God. They inform and instruct creation about God's presence and involvement in the lives of all animated beings and demonstrate the power of gifts that are used in divine purpose.

When the heavenly creature spoke the power of his voice caused the doorposts to shake. This witness demonstrates the power available to those who operate in the purpose of God. One would think that only God could speak with such authority and power to move the doorposts of the temple. However, this witness shows that when you operate in God's purpose for your life, then you are able to speak with the power of God. By denying themselves of self-glory and self-determination and surrendering themselves and their gifts to the service of God, the creatures are able to operate in the power of God and demonstrate glory far above their own.

When the creature shook the doorposts with his honor to the glory of God, the house was filled with smoke indicating the presence of God filling the temple. This is an example of the Shekinah glory or presence of God showing up in a way that causes natural existence to transform, acknowledging His presence and reflecting His glory. Because the seraph was operating in the purpose of God, He empowered the angel's voice in the midst of its worshipful actions. This witness demonstrates how God will empower us to operate in His purpose and will respond to our actions in ways that bring Him honor and reveal His glory to others.

If we deny ourselves and operate in the purpose of God, the Shekinah glory will show up and God will transform the natural existence of our lives to acknowledge His presence and reflect His glory to others. This type of heavenly witness helps us to understand the purpose of our existence and to overcome the illusions of self-grandeur that we inherit through the cursed nature. God will at times use natural occurrences in life to help us discover our giftedness and purpose. The discovery of our giftedness helps us to understand our purpose because we have been given gifts to fulfill that purpose. Dr. Martin Luther King Jr. would not have been the leader he proved to be if he did not have the gift to speak to people in an inspirational manner.

I remember working on a job that required me to transport students to the bus station, hospital, mall, and other recreational activities. Once I was transporting a student to the infirmary and saw a big commotion taking place, but I did not investigate and left the area. Shortly afterwards, I had to transport another student to the infirmary and decided to inquire about what was happening. I discovered that a student had threatened to take his life over a dating relationship gone wrong. The student was standing outside the infirmary but would not go inside, and the counselors were trying to convince him to go in without physical force. After finding out who the student was I asked the safety director if I could talk with the young man. The safety director looked at me as if to say "Who do you think you are?" but then he finally said, "Everyone else has tried. Why not you?"

After a short conservation with the student, I asked him to do me a favor and go into the infirmary for the night. The student said he would do it if I allowed him to get his cigarettes from his room. I told him that I would ask the safety director but could not promise him. The safety director said no as I was sure he would, but I had to try for the student. I went back to the student and asked him if he would spend the night in the infirmary if I promised to bring him his cigarettes. He said yes and turned and walked into the infirmary without incident. I went and got the cigarettes for the student, and he remained in the infirmary without future incidents.

Later that night the safety director came by my office and asked me how I got the student to go into the infirmary after counselors had tried for hours to do so. I told him that I remembered transporting the student the week before and listened to him talk about his situation. Hearing the student share an earlier situation helped me to understand how to reach him in his pain. The safety director stated that he first was opposed to allowing me to try to reach the student after so many professionals had failed and that he did not think I had the training necessary to become involved. He decided that I could not hurt at that point and he did not think I would be able to help the situation, but he was down to his final option of force and wanted to try everything he could before using force. He also informed me that I might have the skills to be a counselor—the kind you cannot receive in training programs.

The incident with the student caused me to reflect on the gifts and abilities within me and helped me discover and respond to my call into ministry. I also began to realize that my being in a position to interact with the student was not an accident. I could see God's hand in the incident and other situations in my life where I was put in a position to be of assistance to people. Through reflection and prayer about these types of situations, God revealed to me that we are given gifts to serve Him by helping each other. Our giftedness is given in relationship to the purpose that God has for our lives—just as the seraphim Isaiah saw were given more than one pair of wings and the ability to speak with the power of God. Without those gifts they would not have been able to deliver the message to Isaiah about serving God with their giftedness for the glory of God and not their own.

The angels not only delivered to Isaiah the message of using his gifts, they also taught him to use his gifts in the service of God. The Bible has other examples of heavenly beings with divine assignments to be heavenly witnesses in the service of God.

God-Servants

In much the same way as the seraphim were assigned to interact with Isaiah, God gave cherubim angels a flaming sword and assigned them to guard the way to the tree of life. Humanity had fallen into sin and was exiled from the Garden of Eden so that they could not get to the tree of life. The flaming sword would have acted against any human who approached the garden because humanity was tainted with sin. Humans were kept from the tree of life because it was designed to give eternal life to them. Sin prevented humanity from being ready to access the tree of life because they would bring death into the eternal continuum. Until Jesus took away our sins, no human could stand at this post. Jesus came that we could have access to the tree of life (Revelation 2:7). Through the blood of Jesus, humanity can be empowered to receive the Flaming Sword to keep the way. Jesus proclaimed this message when He said He makes His ministers a flame of fire (Hebrews 1:7). The sword is the power that truly keeps the way, and the angels stand watch. In the same way, Christians are responsible for standing watch for the body of Christ while God's Word, Spirit, and love work in our lives to keep the way to the tree of life.

The angels assigned to keep the way to the tree of life were those whom God knew would not follow the self-willed influence of the fallen angel Lucifer. They serve as heavenly witnesses for believers because of their obedience to God's will and purpose. God knew their spirit and soul belonged to His will, making them God-servants. These angels were willing to fulfill God's purpose with their lives and could be trusted to guard the way and be armed with the power of the flaming sword. The seraphim were also God-servants and could be trusted with the power to move the doorposts by the sound of their praise. In order for God to trust us with such duties and such power, we must follow the example of the heavenly witnesses and show Him that we are God-servants.

God-servants are willing to give up their personal agendas and accept God's will for their lives. Jesus was a God-servant when He was on the earth. He served humanity in accordance with His Father's will and not the will of humanity (John 14:8-13). He became a part of humanity so that He could serve the will of God through His service to humanity. In His role as God-servant, He did not serve for His glory but rather for the glory of His Father. Because He served for the glory of His Father, His battles became His Father's battles. Jesus' obedience and sacrifice allowed God to establish His glory through His life. We must follow this example in order for the Flaming Sword to become fully active in our lives. The early church experienced the activation of the Flaming Sword after the empowerment of the Holy Spirit. They became instruments of God as they separated themselves from the cursed things (Acts 5:12-16).

The Power of Unity

The power of the sword was not designed to operate in spiritual isolation because it contains attributes of the entire Godhead. For this reason, full activation requires agreement of the body of Christ. The church must operate as the atoms within a magnet. All metals are made up of atoms. However, in most metals the atoms are lined up in different directions rather than in a unified alignment. This disorientation causes the power of one to be cancelled by the power of another. Conversely, the atoms of a magnet are all lined up in the same direction. This arrangement of atoms creates an agreement within the metal and allows the atoms to exert a force that can draw or repel.

When the body of Christ finds the proper agreement in God, we become a force that can draw souls to Christ and repel the cursed things that create division. When we examine the actions of the heavenly witnesses, we see no signs of division among them even though they had different gifts and assignments.

The Flaming Sword is activated in the lives of people in relationship with God through obedience to God, service to God, and love for God. The cherubim were provided with a flaming sword to fulfill the assignment placed on their lives. The power of praise and wings were given to the seraphim to fulfill their assignments. There is no mention in the text of any questions asked by the cherubim or seraphim regarding the assignments they were given. This fact illustrates obedience and love for God on the part of the angels who became the representatives of God at the tree of life and in the life of Isaiah. We must be obedient to God's assignment for our lives. Through obedience we show God that He can trust us to be empowered by His gifts that enable us to fulfill divine purpose.

Chapter 9

Getting Real

Isaiah's Transformation

After seeing God and experiencing the heavenly witnesses, Isaiah was ready to get real with himself, with God, and with others. In getting real with himself, Isaiah reflected on his actions and accepted his faults while confessing his uncleanness. We must accept our faults as a part of the reflective process that leads to divine purpose. Humanity separated itself from the presence of God in an attempt to be self-sufficient. Therefore, it is important and necessary for those seeking purpose to realize and acknowledge their lack of sufficiency and their need for God.

The apostle Paul teaches that in his weakness God makes him strong and perfects His strength through his infirmities (2 Corinthians 12:7-10). Paul helps believers to understand that humans are not designed to be superhuman but rather to depend on the supernatural power of God. Isaiah discovers that he is cut off or destroyed because of the uncleanness of his nature. In realizing that human nature is flawed, insufficient, and cursed, humans are able to reject the notion of self-determination and seek God's help and guidance.

Like Isaiah, when we get real with ourselves we can get real with God and confess that we are in need of His grace. This confession must be an internal spiritual revelation and acceptance as well as a natural proclamation of need and faith (Romans 10:8-10). At this point we are able to shed our notions of self-determination and self-glorification and accept the sufficiency of God's plan, God's will, and God's grace for our lives. This act has the twofold purpose of freeing us from the false hope of grandeur and binds us to the reality of the sufficiency of God's grace.

When we become real with God, we are able to be real with others. In our transformation from destruction to salvation, we become part of the heavenly witness of the gracious will of God. We are able to use our natural design and supernatural favor to help others understand the need to seek God's purpose for their lives. Like Isaiah, we become able to see the flaws of humanity that exist in all humans and help them understand the need to seek God. The best evidence of finding God is indicated in the desire to help others make the same discovery. God is just too good to keep Him to ourselves and must be shared with others.

Isaiah's narrative informs us that he discovered his purpose through his experiences with God. In seeing God exalted and experiencing the heavenly creatures operating in divine purpose, he was able to embrace his own faults and recognize the faults of humanity. This act caused him to cry out to God and receive spiritual cleansing that purged his sin. Once cleansed, Isaiah was able to hear God's voice calling him into divine purpose. The way this narrative is placed in the sixth chapter of Isaiah rather than the first indicates that we often face life experiences before discovering our purpose. However, upon his discovery with God, Isaiah was ready to accept who he was and what he was designed to do. We too are able to discover who we are in God through our experiences with Him, which prepares us to fulfill our destinies.

As in Isaiah's experiences, the discovery of divine purpose requires cleansing and separation from cursed things. The Flaming Sword activates in the lives of believers much like the coal of fire which the angel used to purge Isaiah of his sins. The cleansing process frees believers of the things that separate them from the presence of God and distract them from their purpose. This process also allows believers to clearly receive God's revelations of divine purpose and spiritual empowerment for destiny.

Jesus is the ultimate heavenly witness for all to see how one in the flesh can be a God-servant and fulfill divine purpose. The Flaming Sword was active in His life as He spoke to people He influenced. His words of life separated them from the cursed things of death. This power of separation from death was illustrated when Jesus told the man with leprosy to be clean (Matthew 8:3); the legion of devils to come out of the man (Matthew 8:32); the woman with the issue of blood that her faith made her whole (Matthew 9:22); the girl to rise from death (Luke 8:54); the man to take up his bed and walk (John 5:6-9); the man with palsy that his sins were forgiven (Luke 5:19-20); and Lazarus to come forth from death (John 11:42-44).

Such power to separate humanity from the influence of sin and death is illustrated throughout the life and ministry of Jesus. His life was the example of how humanity without sin is able to speak the things of life and separate others from the cursed things that prevent eternal life. Eternal life is not something that humanity had to achieve; rather it is what humanity lost in following the words of death spoken by the devil through the serpent (Revelation 12:9). Jesus became the embodiment of the Word of God in flesh so that He could speak the words that separate humanity for the curse of death and bring us back into the presence of God.

One of the many reasons the sword was active in the life of Jesus was because He always focused on His Father's Word and purpose even though He was the Word made flesh. The Word of God is described as being sharper than any two-edged sword, with the power to separate between the marrow and the bone, between the thoughts and discernment of the heart (Hebrews 4:12). As Jesus spoke the words of His Father He brought forward life into a world of darkness and sin. As Christians we are expected to follow His example so that our lives could be illuminated with the truth of God's presence, His relationship with us, and His will for our lives.

Through Jesus we are able to reverse the steps taken by fallen humanity to separate from God. First, Jesus has removed the shame of sin so that we can stop hiding from God. We can move back toward God and enter into His presence, allowing Him to restore the relationship we once had with Him. The Holy Scriptures instruct us that God invited us back into His presence through the sacrifice of

Jesus the Christ (John 3:15-21). If we are estranged from God in any way, we need to return to His presence. As we move toward God, we will find that the hindrances in our lives will not follow us.

After deciding to return to God, we can get real enough to stop making excuses for our wrongdoings and repent of our sins. As we move toward God His influence helps us to stop rationalizing our actions through human reasoning and seek spiritual guidance. God's influence enables us to repent of the things that interfere with our relationship, fellowship, and service to God (Hebrews 4:14-16). The Spirit of God influences us to seek Him, and He responds to our seeking by revealing Himself and His true will for our lives.

It is important to remember that we cannot take a humanistic path if we want to enter into the presence of a spiritual God. The destination we seek requires us to find the way to transcend the human reality and take a spiritual journey. Several key scriptures give us directions as to how we can make such a transformation. It all begins with God as He indicated that: "For God so loved the world that he gave his only begotten son so that whosoever believes in him shall not perish but have everlasting life" (John 3:16). The journey began in heaven with God moved by His love for humanity so much that He became flesh and came to redeem us to Himself. In response to God's action we must: "Seek first the kingdom of God and its righteousness and all things will be added to our lives" (Matthew 6:33). We must seek and establish a personal relationship with Jesus Christ as our Lord and Savior and place our focus on the things of God for our lives.

Once we have a relationship with Christ it is important that we "be not conformed to the ways of this world but be transformed by the renewing of our minds" (Romans 12:2). We must resist the humanistic spirit that tempts us to believe our destiny is in our hands and that we are sufficient in ourselves. We must allow our minds to be renewed spiritually by God's Word and God's Spirit and resist the temptation to try to live independent of God. It is important that we do not lean to our own understanding but in all of our ways acknowledge Him, and He will direct our path (Proverbs 3:5-6).

The Continuum of Life

In getting real with God, Jesus activates the power of the Flaming Sword in our lives and allows us to share the continuum of life that exists in the presence of God. The tree of life represents this continuum of life. In it all beings share life, holiness, and love in every aspect of their eternal existence. This is the place of perfect healing and blessing that we as Christians strive for. This is the continuum that Jesus invited us into when He said that He came that we might have life and have it more abundantly. The continuum of life is illustrated in Revelation 21 and 22. The fruit of the tree from which we are to eat is life itself that abides continually in the presence of God. The flaming sword was brought forward to keep the way of this continuum of life with God, kept from the sin that caused humanity's separation from God.

The unholy things that came forward because of sin are not designed to live forever. The Flaming Sword operates in us to separate the unholy things of the world from the eternal living spirit that is within us. Through Jesus Christ we are given access to the presence of God and eternal life. God has given humanity access into His presence, but He has not given access to the unholy and cursed things that we receive from the world. The Flaming Sword is designed to separate our spiritual lives (souls) from the taint of sin and unrighteousness. This Flaming Sword, which consists of the Word, Spirit, and love of God, separates the eternal souls of humanity from the things that bring death (separation from God).

Life is a continuum (something capable of being shared infinitely) that came forth out of God and exists in God's presence as well as in those who abide within His presence (Revelation 4:6-11). This position is illustrated in the scripture that identifies Jesus as the Alpha and the Omega, the Beginning and the End (Revelation 1:8, 17-18). Those who abide in the presence of God share this continuum with God, and therefore they have eternal life with God. This is why the cursed things and sin can't abide in His presence, because those who abide in Him share the continuum. We become a part of God and He becomes a part of us as illustrated when Jesus said, "I am in the Father and the Father is in me, and if you have seen the Father you have seen me" (John 14:7-13). Though He was a man

He could abide in the continuum because He was without sin. This theme is illustrated in John 14 and 15.

Sinners can't abide in the presence of God because they are tainted by sin, which would contaminate the continuum that is shared by all who abide within the presence of God. God will not allow the continuum to be contaminated; therefore, He moves the tainted things from His presence and cleanses His children so that we may return without the contamination of sin. The Flaming Sword becomes the agent of separation God uses to keep the children from the cursed things after they have been washed in the blood of Jesus. We remember that our parents would not allow us to go back outside to play after we took our bath for the evening. Just as we were not allowed to go back to our former activities that caused us to become filthy physically, we must remain in the house of God and avoid the filth that we played in before we were saved. Those who abide in the house of God remain in the continuum through the blood of Jesus and benefit from the spiritual life that God shares with His children.

The Flaming Sword is not some mystical force to be sought after and controlled by humanity. This sword is not a thing; rather it is an extension of the presence of God that contains His attributes. When God gave the sword to the angels in the Garden of Eden, the angels became the representatives of God in that place and time. The angels were not assigned to keep the way to the tree of life without divine empowerment; rather the sword became the empowerment they needed to fulfill His purpose. Just as God empowered the angels, He also empowers humanity in our assignment to overcome the cursed things of the world and to enter into His presence. God is the only judge who is able to separate the cursed things from that which is holy, and He has extended Himself into the lives of fallen humanity because of His desire to have us commune with Him and fulfill our purpose.

In the operation of the Flaming Sword there is an agreement between God's Word, Spirit, and love that empowers humanity to fulfill its purpose. It is important for believers to receive as much of God's Word as possible so that the agreement between the Word and the Spirit grows and brings our lives into agreement with God. When we agree with God, we are alive and able to receive the revelations of God. We cannot know the things of God through our natural intellectual process. They are inwardly discerned when the Word of God and the Spirit of God merge together. God is also able to illuminate the lives of others with His revelations as we allow our light to shine through our obedient witness to His Word (Matthew 5:14-16). As living witnesses we are able to share the God that is within us with others.

Being

Theologian Paul Tillich stated that God is being itself. He described God as the power of being which is within every human being, enabling them to exist and without which they would cease to exist.[2] As a result, God is not apart from the world, but rather the world is a medium of His continuing activity. God shared this sense of being with humanity as He placed the breath of life in man and he became a living soul (Genesis 2:7). This act of creation brought forth humans, who are different from all other earthly creatures. This sense of being placed humanity in a relationship of communion with God and with one another. Humanity was created with a spiritual, holy, and righteous nature that was similar to the nature of God.

After the fall of the first humans in the garden, humanity received a cursed nature that is split from the essence of humanity. The essence of humanity refers to what God intended for us to be. In the choice of "being" separate from God, humanity received a sense of being less than what they originally received and became dead to God. The only other human to live in the original existence was Jesus, who is described by theologians such as Tillich as the New Being. He is described as such because He portrayed completely what God meant for humanity to be. As a result, God was able to fully act through Jesus as He planned to act through humanity, even to the point of saving humanity. There was an unlimited supply of *being* in Jesus to share with all of humanity so that our sense of being was elevated to being alive to God. Tillich saw love as a power rather than an emotion. The revelation of Christ emphasizes love as the law of God. For only God's love has the power to unite that which has been separated, God and humanity.

Activity of the Flaming Sword

Jesus illustrated that the sword is empowered by love as He used this power to separate humanity from the bondage of Satan, the power of the law, and the curse of sin and death. The sword brings death to whatever separates us from God and allows us to remain in the continuum of life with God. The sword becomes active in the lives of God-servants who are driven by the love of God and humanity in the fulfillment of divine purpose.

In one community where I served as pastor a partially abandoned house less than five blocks from the church became a place for crack addicts and prostitutes to hang out and commit acts of sin. The prostitutes would walk the streets in front of the church, and the drug addicts were going in and out to get high. The house soon became known as the "House of Pain" because of all the pain and suffering that came about because of the actions of those who went there. The actions of the people gathering at the "House of Pain" certainly were not in agreement with the will of God; therefore they were bringing suffering on themselves and the people around them within the community. After discussing the situation with the church and asking the church to pray with me, God led us to conduct drive-by prayers each time we drive past the house.

We realized that the people gathering at the house were not our enemy, but the spirits that drove them to dwell in this place of sin and death were our enemy. This revelation allowed us to love the people who we being held captive by the spirits operating in the House of Pain. These spirits had become united in their efforts to destroy the community through drug addiction, sex, and crime. We continuously conducted drive-by prayers as we asked God to remove the building that had become a house for spirits that were thriving and destroying the people within the community. Soon after we began our drive-by prayers, the owners of the property allowed the fire department to burn the house down during a training process to help train new firefighters.

The firefighters used the tool of fire to destroy the house that was uniting evil and causing pain within the community. In similar fashion, Christians become agents through which the power of God flows to help people become separated from cursed habits in their lives. The morning the house was finally burned down, God told me to drive through the area. When I saw the ashes from the building that once was the home of so many evil spirits, I began to shout halleluiah and praises to God. I was excited to see the power of God operating in the hearts of the owners and the firefighters to separate the abode of evil from the community.

When the sword is active in our lives it removes the cursed things that separate us from life in abundance. The cursed things cannot stop God from blessing us but they can block our reception of the blessings from the Lord and leave us exposed to the influence of sin and death. Sickness, death, depression, hatred, poverty, violence, and division are all influences of the cursed things. When the sword is active in our lives we become separated from the influence of such things.

I remember a church member who would go on weekend crack binges and was about to lose his marriage. As his wife was packing her things getting ready to depart, he asked her to do one last thing for him. He acknowledged that he had no right to make this request. He informed her that if she did not get the results she was expecting he would help her pack her bags. She said, "What is this one last thing you want me to do so that I can get you out of my life?" He told her to take him to his pastor's house. They called me to see if it was okay for them to come by for a visit. I told them to come, not sure of the reason for their visit until they began to share the situation with my wife and me.

While we were sitting at the breakfast table discussing the situation, the Spirit of the Lord led us to pray. During our prayer I felt the power of God begin to activate in the life of this husband and break the yoke of bondage. The reality of loss in his life allowed him to see that he had to make the choice between allowing the cursed things to remain in his life and lose his family and bring death upon himself or choosing a life in Christ and redeem his life and family. Realizing that he was about to lose his family, whom he loved very much, we were able to get him to focus on the love of God. In sharing inspirations through Scripture and prayer, we were able to get him to trust and believe in God's Word. Through prayer we were able to help him to open up and allow the power of the Holy Spirit to intercede in his situation. We became the heavenly witnesses that God allowed this brother to look on and somehow see past our humanity and see God for His deliverance. Once freed of the darkness of Satan's influence, this brother was able to discover his purpose of existence.

Through the activation of the Word of God, the Spirit of God, and the love of God this young man overcame the influence of the cursed things. He walked away from drugs, became active in the church, and he and his wife both answered their call into ministry. This same young man is now a pastor, and the two of them are leading people to Christ. He looks ten years younger than he did ten years ago because he is now free to walk in the abundance of life that renews us day by day. Because the Flaming Sword was active in the lives of my wife and me, we were able to help someone else activate the power of God in their lives. Just as God shared His sense of being with humanity, in Jesus we are able to share the power that God invests within us to help others walk in the fulfillment of God's will for their lives.

Unit 4

Accepting Divine Purpose

Spiritual Principle: So let it be, according to your word.

Chapter 10

Facing the Contents of the Cup

Facing Your Humanity

M any times in biblical reading we do not see the human struggle that people undergo in their experiences with God and the world. The Bible characters are in defeat in one paragraph and have won the battle and celebrated the victory in the next. The book of Matthew gives a vivid illustration of human struggle in accepting divine purpose in Jesus' garden experience (Matthew 26:36-46). It is interesting to note that both Adam and Jesus (the second Adam) were tested in a garden, and both struggles involved accepting divine purpose. Adam's failure made Jesus' test necessary, and the outcome of both trials affected all of humanity (1 Corinthians 15:20-22).

Unlike Adam and all other humans, Jesus did not struggle with discovering His divine purpose on earth. The Scriptures clearly indicate that Jesus knew His purpose even as a child. After being left in the temple, His parents questioned Him and He told them He had to be about His Father's business. This passage indicates that Jesus knew of His Father and was aware of His purpose to His Father (Luke 2:41-52). He also realized the authority of His heavenly Father had precedence over the authority of His earthly parents.

In His adult ministry, Jesus gave many references to understanding His divine purpose on earth. He informed the disciples that He would suffer and die but would rise on the third day. Jesus illustrated an understanding of His death and resurrection by indicating that He would raise the temple in three days after it was destroyed. Jesus also seemed to understand the timing of His purpose. When His mother requested that He help the people at the wedding feast, He informed her that it was not His time. After working miracles in people lives He would ask them not to reveal it at that time.

People such as John the Baptist demonstrated some under-standing of Jesus' purpose on earth. John introduced Jesus to his disciples as the "Lamb of God who came to take away the sins of the world" (John 1:29-34). John also stated that he was a witness for Jesus and responsible for preparing the people to receive Jesus' message of salvation. He also indicated that Jesus would baptize believers with the Holy Spirit and fire. Peter also received revela-tions of Jesus' purpose in indicating that He was the Christ and the Son of the living God (Matthew 16:13-20). Jesus stated that these revelations came from God the Father, which informs us that God is involved in our process of accepting divine purpose. It is helpful to know that we are not on our own as the serpent tried to suggest in the Garden of Eden.

In Jesus' garden trial experience, He uses the metaphor of a cup to represent His purpose in God. In this discourse, Jesus seemed to examine what was in the cup and found it distasteful, displeasing, and distressful. Because of the contents of the cup, Jesus became deeply sorrowful and distressed. The cup contained the flawed con-dition of humanity which was filled with sin, it contained suffering, and it also contained death, which involved being separated from God. In the garden Jesus struggled with the idea of receiving the contents of the cup.

In Jesus' struggles He had to face His humanity, which knew no sin. However, one of His purpose-related assignments involved receiving the sins of humanity. Jesus had never been intimate with sin. He knew that He had to become sin in order for us to become the righteousness of God in Him (Romans 5:21). Jesus realized that humanity is in a flawed condition under the curse of sin and death. In order to fulfill God's purpose for His life He would have to embrace this flawed condition of humanity and the sins associated with it.

The reality of accepting this flawed condition caused Jesus' soul to be sorrowful unto death.

This would be the first and only time Jesus experienced the flawed condition of humanity. He was capable of sinning but chose not to sin. Jesus was not born with original sin, which is passed through the seed of man, and He did not commit actual sin in His human condition. In His struggles Jesus asked His Father to allow the cup to pass from Him and find another way. In this request Jesus demonstrated His humanity, which has the capacity to fail, but He used the relationship with His Father to overcome that tendency of humanity.

Like Jesus we have to face our flawed humanity and the sins associated with it. We have to face the original state of sin we inherited from Adam. This state causes us to be flawed, makes us prone to failure, and renders us subject to the forces of evil. Our own sins add to our condition and make us more susceptible to the curse of death. In accepting God's will for our lives we have to come to the understanding and acceptance that we are not able to accomplish that will on our own. In coming to this realization we reverse the actions of Adam and Eve, surrender our state of independence, and become more dependent of God. This is why we must confess our sins and ask God to save us and guide us through our human existence.

When we surrender our independence and honor God as Lord of our lives, we begin to walk in the newness of life with Christ. In this newness we are empowered by God to overcome the flaws of our human condition. If the mighty Jesus found that facing the human condition caused Him to grieve, then we cannot expect everything in fulfilling God's will for our lives to be easy. However, we must expect God to see us through as He saw Jesus through. In accepting God's help with our human condition we acknowledge that there is something wrong with us and reject the demonic notion of self-transformation offered to Eve in the Garden. Through such acceptance, we are better prepared to accept the purpose-related assignments in our lives.

Facing Your Suffering

In the Garden of Gethsemane, Jesus realized that drinking from the cup involved suffering. He understood that He would die a painful death in which His body would be broken and His blood would be shed for the hope of all humanity. His sweat fell to the ground like drops of blood, indicating the agony of the flesh He was experiencing. Much like our flesh, Jesus' flesh did not want to endure suffering, but His Spirit was willing. He cried out to His heavenly Father concerning the condition of His flesh. In facing His humanity, Jesus realized that He needed the help of His Father to fulfill His purpose in life.

We too must face suffering in our journey of life, and we strive to accept God's will for our lives. We also must call on our heavenly Father through our big brother Jesus. The suffering of Jesus gave us power to endure and overcome the conditions of suffering we experience. The breaking of His body gave us healing power over sickness of all kinds (by His stripes we are healed). The brokenness of Jesus makes us whole and empowered to overcome the conditions of human suffering. We must realize that all humans are broken and have been that way since Adam. Because we are broken we are in need of God to bring wholeness in our lives.

The shedding of His blood cleanses us of sin and gives us power over unrighteousness and the principalities of evil. Through the blood of Jesus our relationship with God is changed and we can cry out "Abba Father." We have to accept that we cannot save ourselves and must accept the blood of Jesus as the cleansing agent for our souls. In this acceptance God is able to empower us to escape the spiritual sickness of sin while we strive to fulfill our purpose. This empowerment also enables us to complete the purpose-related assignments of our lives.

Facing Death

Jesus had to face the death of His human existence, but He understood that His divine existence would continue after that death. Jesus, knowing that His Father is holy, also understood that to drink of the cup of sin would cause separation (death) between Him and His Father. In all His existence as the Word of God (John 1:1) and the Son of God (John 1:14), Jesus had never been separated from His Father. In this experience, Jesus struggled to accept His death. The separation from His Father was the main suffering that Jesus asked His Father to allow to pass. This struggle clearly indicates the humanity of Christ. However, it also indicates that Jesus was willing to endure the experience of death to redeem creation.

The garden experience indicates that Jesus was aware of His purpose but struggled with acceptance of that purpose. As with Jesus, our acceptance of divine purpose requires some degree of death in our lives. It often requires the death of relationships, lifestyles, careers, and carnal habits that we enjoy. In facing our destiny and the fulfillment of divine purpose we struggle with the notion of death (separation) from things that we have come to know and love. The reality of giving up things we love and find pleasurable and profitable can be distressful for us. Like Jesus we find ourselves asking that the cup be taken from us. I remember God instructing me to give up my career in education after I had gained success, credibility, and financial gain. The idea of leaving the job I worked hard for and enjoyed was not easy for me. It was only after giving up the career that I began to understand what God was trying to show me and how He would provide for obedient servants.

In the garden experience, Jesus asks three of His disciples, His innermost circle, to pray with Him through His time of struggle. But their flesh got the best of them and they went to sleep on Him three times. This discourse illustrates the isolation that is often experienced in facing and accepting divine purpose. Others around us seem unable and at times unwilling to feel or understand our pain. It is the struggles in the flesh of our friends that makes it difficult for them to assist us in our struggles of acceptance (Matthew 26:40-41). Jesus had to struggle in isolation with His desire to avoid the difficult reality of His death (separation from God).

Many people struggle with the aspects of death that are necessary in accepting divine purpose and face their struggle in some form of isolation. Like Jesus we must beseech God to empower and guide us through this struggle. We must come to understand it is a struggle between our divine nature and our carnal nature, because like Jesus we possess both natures within one being. Our divine nature wants to do the will of God while our carnal nature wants to avoid sacrifice and separation (death). The struggle is one of choice as to whether we choose the divine nature or the carnal nature as the destiny of our lives.

In the acceptance of divine purpose we have to learn to admit our state of sinfulness, which exists in our fleshly nature. By coming to terms with our sinful nature, we are able to confess that we transgress against the law and the will of God and need His help for salvation. This confession involves rejecting the cursed and carnal nature we are born in and accepting God's choice for our existence. In this confession, we have to make the choice just like Adam and Jesus did in their garden experiences. We have the choice of self-glorification and self-determination of our human nature, or we can embrace the destiny God has our existence that lives through our divine nature (Ephesians 1:3-6). This is where the power of the gospel leads us to our moment of salvation and empowers us to embrace the divine purpose for our lives. The Word of God says that through faith in Jesus we are able to live according to the will of God (Romans 1:16-17).

Chapter 11

Reaching God

Praying in Isolation

In the Garden of Gethsemane, God never said anything in response to Jesus' repeated petition to let the cup pass, and Jesus' friends did not prove to be of any help in the matter. His friends kept going to sleep on Him even after He asked them repeatedly to pray with Him. They seemed to be dealing with sorrow of their own and were not able to be of much help to Jesus. In the midst of His isolation and torment He prayed to His Father. He knew that His only solace would be found in reaching God because His flesh was struggling with His divine destiny and His friends were of little support or encouragement. In prayer, Jesus reached heaven and God sent an angel to strengthen Him. In studying the Scriptures, we notice that the angel did not attempt to change the course of events or to change Jesus' situation to get Him out. Rather, the angel prepared Him to go through His ordeal.

Sometimes we have to isolate ourselves or be isolated in order to reach God. God allows us to be placed where we are not distracted by the misguided advice of others when He is preparing us for the fulfillment of our journey. It is good to spend time alone with God in prayer so that we can be real with ourselves and God about our situations. Sometimes our deliverance involves going through the struggles we face in life. Often we try to change people and their situations or try to get them out of their situations when it is necessary for them to go through in preparation for their destiny.

If you help a butterfly break out of its cocoon, you stop the struggle that will build the wing muscles needed for flight. Upon being released from the cocoon, the butterfly would be unable to fulfill its divine purpose because it became crippled through good intentions. At times God allows people to pray in isolation to prepare them for the task ahead. Sometimes our role is only to strengthen people in their garden experiences with encouragement and support of presence. To interfere with the process can cause long-lasting harm and hinder their spiritual development.

Praying Through Torment

While Jesus prayed to God His soul was in torment, to the point that He felt like dying and His sweat became like great drops of blood (Luke 22:43-44). Both the human and divine natures of Jesus struggled with the destiny of the cross. Jesus' human nature would have to endure horrific physical suffering to be broken for humanity. Jesus' divine nature would have to endure the spiritual suffering of separation from the Father in order to receive the sins of the world. However, through His torment Jesus keep His focus on the will of God for His life.

Jesus did not make excuses for His situation when He could have because we were the cause of Him being there. Even in His rejection of a destiny of suffering He spoke to God out of His relationship with Him. He remembered that God was His Father and cared about Him even when He was suffering. Jesus demonstrated faith in God and His relationship with Him during His time of torment. It was in His torment that He reached heaven and God sent an angel to minister to Him. Jesus' faith was rewarded by God's assistance even when He did not get His request granted.

In our times of torment we may be in situations that appear unfair and unbearable, but we have to learn to trust the wisdom of God for our lives. Talking to God in sincerity helps us to get beyond the excuses of our lives and learn to trust Him. Like Jesus we have to understand that some situations of life require us to place ourselves and our trust totally in God. It is important for us to remember our relationship with God and speak as His children rather than as those who have no hope. In talking as children of God we engage our divine nature in the process of reaching God. The Bible teaches us that God will not deny Himself, and thus He will respond to our needs even when we cannot have our desires.

Our flesh tends to focus on the suffering and loss, but the divine nature within us is able to focus on the will of God. It is our divine nature that allows us to keep faith in God in times of torment, and our prayers reach heaven. The Word teaches us that when we pray in humility, seek His faith, and repent for our evil, He will hear us from heaven and heal our land. When we reach heaven God responds to our need and visits us through His many ways of blessing. We must pray to Him in faith through our relationship as sons and daughters because of Jesus Christ. God's response is not one of merit pay; rather it is a response of love through the relationship He has with us.

Praying with Fervor

When Jesus found Himself isolated in His torment, He reached out to God more earnestly in prayer. If we pray with sincerity, fervor, and faith we will be able to reach God and engage the divine power in helping us to overcome our flesh. As Jesus engaged the divine power through His fervent prayer time, we too can engage the divine power. The Bible teaches that the fervent prayers of a righteous person avail much (James 5:13-18). God is waiting for His children to reach out to Him because He wants to reveal Himself to us, inform us of our divine purpose, and empower us to fulfill that purpose.

Remember that God wanted Jesus to be successful in accepting His purpose, and He wants us to be successful in accepting our own divine purpose. Because God wants us to be successful, He will allow us to engage His power to go through our times of struggle. God will not remove us from our struggles when He knows they are needed to prepare us to fulfill our purpose. God often develops the abilities and attitudes of people while they are living rebellious and sinful lives. He uses the experiences of life to prepare us for the struggles involved in our fulfillment of purpose-related assignments.

God will send who or what is needed to strengthen us through our struggle. However, He does it in a way that lets us know we need His assistance. Many times we try to resolve our problems through our physical resources when they require spiritual engagement. In these times God puts us or allow us to be placed in situations where our physical resources are not available or not able to accomplish the task. Like Jesus we are forced to reach out through our spirit and engage God's heavenly assistance. Jesus' garden experience helped to prepare Him for the journey to the cross. God sent Him what He needed to fulfill the divine purpose placed on His life. God will also give us what we need in our times of struggle and use those times to prepare us for our divine purpose.

Chapter 12

Embracing Destiny

Accepting Who You Are

God never gave Jesus an answer to His repeated petition to pass the cup, indicating that Jesus already had the answer within Himself. This suggests that Jesus' struggle was not in seeking His purpose but rather in accepting some of the assignments of that purpose and how they would affect His life. Because He had the answer within Himself, He only needed heavenly support to prepare for the assignments of divine purpose.

A big part of accepting divine purpose involves accepting the assignments that come with the purpose. This process could be called *embracing destiny*, which involves realizing who we are, accepting the assignments related to who we are, and accepting God's will for our lives.

In the midst of Jesus' struggles to embrace His destiny, His relationship with His Father helped Him in His understanding and acceptance. First, Jesus realized and accepted who He was. He was God's Son and His Christ, the chosen Messiah, the Word of God who came in the flesh to save humanity. Jesus knew He was the only human in existence born free of sin and the only one to live free of sin since Adam sinned in the garden. Therefore, He could abide and operate in the fullness of the presence and power of God. There was nothing within Him, even His flesh, for the enemy to condemn or to hinder Him from being with God. He was born without the limitations of sin, and the law had no power over Him. Jesus understood that He was God and human at the same time. In order to discover who we are we must do as John did in writing the genealogy of Jesus. The Gospel of John traces Jesus' lineage back to God rather than to Abraham.

Jesus also focused on the fact that He, as the "Son of Man," came from His Father rather than from His mother or Joseph. He focused on the supernatural lineage of His Father rather than the limited lineage of His mother. Jesus understood that even though He was in the flesh He was the Son of His heavenly Father. We must focus on this heavenly lineage in our struggles with identifying who we are. In doing this we understand that the lineage of Abraham is a cursed lineage and therefore limited and subject to the law. Abraham's righteousness was imputed unto him, which indicates that the righteousness that comes through Jesus was extended to him early. It is like being paroled from prison early on good behavior. We must trace our lineage beyond that of our forebears and connect with our origin.

It's important for us to realize that we were created by the Word of God, the one who is the Alpha and the Omega (Revelation 1:8). This concept helps us to realize that we originated in God and are designed to end in God. In understanding the Alpha and Omega (beginning and end) concept we are better able to accept the fact that we were created to emulate God in the earthly realm. We were created in the image and likeness of God and given dominion over the earth and all the creatures of the earth (Genesis 1:27-28). Humans were commanded to subdue the earth and to fill it by increasing humanity. God does not command anything to do something unless it has the abilities to do so with Him. This helps us to realize that we were designed to overcome all things in the earth realm and abide in the presence of God.

Remember, it was the Spirit of God that animated Adam's body. We are spirits that live in flesh. This helps us to focus on operating as spiritual beings rather than entrapping ourselves through the pleasures of the flesh. A friend once told me, "If you know the purpose of a thing then you know the potential of a thing." In discovering what

God intended us to be and accomplish we discover our potential. The devil's deception in the garden involved the loss of awareness of potential. The enemy convinced humanity to give up the infinite knowledge, wisdom, understanding, and power of being dependent upon God for the false independence of the finite abilities of the flesh. The potential of humanity can only be released through our relationship with God. This is knowledge that the devil does not want us to remember, and without it we perish.

Understanding the concept of relationship and potential is the lesson of the David and Goliath story. The soldiers that David visited saw themselves as the army of Israel. They were afraid to face Goliath because they were looking to their natural potential to fight the battle. The enemy often wins battles that we have the potential to win because we do not operate in relationship with God. David realized that he was a soldier in the army of the Lord, and therefore he looked to his supernatural potential. By realizing that he was in God's army he understood that the battle was for God to win and him to fight. This awareness of relationship and potential gave David power over his fear and power over the enemy.

Christ came to give us back the knowledge of who we are in God (children of God) with the potential to fulfill the will of God for our lives. Jesus reminds us that we are overcomers and thus able to overcome all things through the power of God within us. Through our relationship with Christ we rediscover that we are joint-heirs to the kingdom of God. We begin to understand our potential to subdue the things of the earth realm. Living as children of God, we are better prepared to overcome the temptations of demonic forces and remain focused on our purpose in life.

Accepting Purpose-Related Assignments

Secondly, Jesus realized and accepted the assignments involved in Him being the Christ. As the Christ He would be betrayed by His own, suffer at the hand of His accused, be crucified, receive the sins of the world, and die on the cross. Jesus realized that His Father had prepared Him for these assignments, and the knowledge helped to sustain Him in His struggles. He understood that He had been given gifts that would allow Him to overcome the trials of His assignments. Jesus knew He had the ability to forgive sin and that He was life and resurrection itself. Therefore, He understood He had the power and knowledge to overcome all that went with His assignments. Similar to the experiences of Jesus, believers have to accept assignments that are related to our purpose. In acceptance of purpose-related assignments we have to become aware of the gifts God has given us to fulfill those assignments.

The understanding of assignments and gifts are also expressed in the David and Goliath story. David knew that as a soldier of God's army, he was sent to stand against the enemy when the other soldiers were afraid. David also understood that his own giftedness had prepared him for the battle. David refused the king's armor because he knew that he was not gifted and prepared for such a fight. Being experienced as a shepherd, David was prepared to use the sling. He understood that God allows us to fulfill our divine assignments through the giftedness He has given and prepared us for. Knowing this, David armed himself with weapons that complemented his gifts and preparations.

Esther also faced a divine assignment that placed her in jeopardy. When King Ahasuerus signed an executive order to destroy the Jews, Mordecai asked Esther to petition the king on the Jews' behalf. Mordecai's request was contrary to the traditions and laws of the land and required Esther to put her life on the line to save her people. Esther understood through the words of Mordecai that God was the one who would deliver the Jews and only required someone to stand for His people. Esther asked the Jews to fast with her and resolved to use the giftedness God had given her and the preparation she had received in order to gain the king's favor. She put on her royal apparel and went to see the king unrequested. Esther's appearance and disposition captured the king's attention and won his favor. Through her humility and ingenuity, God gave Haman over into Esther's hand and he lost his head on his own gallows and the Jews were delivered.

In preparing for our divine assignments we must discover the gifts that God has given to us. We must also go through our time of preparation in which God allows us to develop talents and abilities that are needed to fulfill our assignments. As with David and Esther,

God begins preparing us for our assignments long before we have to face them. Our talents and abilities are manifestations of the spiritual and natural gifts that God has placed in our lives. In learning these talents and abilities, we become more aware and prepared for the types of assignments that are associated with our divine purpose.

In my personal life, I know that one of my assignments is to pastor. In examination of my experiences and abilities, I realize that God has given me what is needed to serve as an effective pastor. I have a compassion for people, the ability to listen, and the ability to help people share personal concerns. These abilities are important for a pastor to meet the needs of a congregation. If you do not like people and have no patience for their troubles, then you do not have the necessary skills to be an effective pastor. I once interviewed a young lady for a job at a daycare center who told me that she did not like dealing with children. I informed her that she was applying for the wrong job.

In knowing our gifts and understanding the talents and abilities that manifest through those gifts, we become better prepared to fulfill the divine assignments of our destiny. Having the ability to share information in an organized manner that can be understood by a variety of people is important for someone assigned to be a teacher. Our talents and abilities are indicators of what potential assignments God has planned for our lives. The talents and abilities we possess also help to ensure that we are prepared to complete these assignments. This is important because demonic forces attempt to place false assignments into our lives. We often spend a lot of time and effort trying to be something we were not designed to be. In this manner the enemy deceives us into using our giftedness for activities that are counterproductive to our purpose and the will of God.

Many drug dealers are gifted to be successful business persons. However, due to environmental conditions, demonic influence, personal greed, and rebellion toward God, many gifted persons are using their abilities to harm the kingdom of God. We see the entrepreneur spirit at work in rappers who were in the drug game and later develop successful businesses with their money and influence. One of the most striking examples of this concept occurred in the life of Stanley Tukey Williams. Stanley was one of the founding members of the deadly street gang known as the Crips. While on death row Stanley became an author of children's books that sold well, even while he was in prison. The gifts of leadership and inspiring people were always in Stanley, but forces in his early life led him to use those gifts to inspire people to a life of violence and crime that spread across the nation. The enemy snares young gifted persons who have not discovered their divine purpose and places false assignments in their lives to entrap them away from their true destiny.

The enemy even tried to trap Jesus into needlessly trying God, exalting Himself, and worshiping the devil. Even in human flesh, Jesus' awareness of who He was in God empowered Him when dealing with Satan's failed attempts at deception. In accepting who He was Jesus also realized the assignments that His Father planned for His earthly existence. Unlike the rest of humanity, Jesus also realized that no one else could do His work. If God let Him pass the cup there was no one else who could drink from it, and all humanity would be lost (Matthew 26:50-54).

Accepting God's Will Above Our Own

Finally, Jesus placed God's will above His own and accepted what the Father predetermined for His earthly life (John 18:11). In embracing His destiny Jesus was willing to give up all in His *natural* existence for the sake of the *spiritual* existence of all. Jesus embraced His divine nature in order to overcome the temptations of His flesh. We also have natural and divine natures operating within us. We are spiritual beings suffering through the curse of human existence within a cursed world. It is within our divine natures that we connect with the presence and power of God. We must learn to embrace our divine nature because that is where we find the purpose for our natural existence. In embracing who we are, we become aware and more prepared for the work that God has for our lives. We begin to understand that not fulfilling our divine assignments can cause great loss for ourselves and the kingdom of God. Unlike Jesus, God can use others to do our work, but there is still loss if we neglect it (Esther 4:13-14). In realizing who we are and what our work is we must place God's will above our own.

Our obedience to God's assignments for our lives puts us in the service of the Lord. As we serve God we become His representatives in the areas of our assignments. It is important to remember that God will empower and protect those who represent Him. The battle is not ours; it belongs to Him. We must remember that God is assigning us for the glory of His kingdom. We are not to choose our own assignment or to establish our own will, but we must surrender to the will of God, who called us into our assignments of service. As God-servants, we are to represent His honor, glory, and name by denying ourselves and walking in submission to His will for our lives. As we walk in submission, God will empower us to fulfill our assignments. This empowerment activates the Flaming Sword within us so that we can keep the way to the tree of life.

Through our submission to God's will, we learn to love God with all of our heart, mind, soul, and strength. Love is the most important aspect of embracing our destiny. God's acts of creating, separating, covering, instructing, and redeeming humanity were all motivated by His love. When our actions are motivated by our love for God, love for humanity, and love for the kingdom of God, then we are empowered to represent and serve the kingdom. As servants of the kingdom, we are empowered with the Flaming Sword to keep the way to the tree of life wherever we are assigned to serve.

The love of God is the key to activating the power of God in our lives. God can't entrust us with His power if we do not operate in love. We must learn to love God in order to obey Him and serve Him. In learning to love God we are transformed into children of God and take on His attributes, which are empowered by love. The love of God is the secret to Christian living, overcoming the world, and eternal life. We are not able to give up the desires of the flesh, the selfish nature of our free will, or the influence of evil spirits without loving God. Without the love of God we are unable to love and submit ourselves to one another without abuse occurring. It is the love of God that empowers us to walk according to the Word and be submissive to the guidance of the Holy Spirit within us. Love is the true power that makes the difference between the children of God and the unholy creations that were given over to their own self-will and ungodly desires.

God is represented only by those who are in relationship with Him. As God-servants we represent God when we allow Him to occupy the emptiness within us and transform us into what He created us to be. Surrendering to God is necessary for this type of spiritual filling to occur because God does not abide where He is not welcome. We must be in a right and holy relationship with God through Jesus Christ in order to have the sword activated in our lives and become God-servants. The relationship God intended for us is one in which He lives within us and we become like Him, living in the presence and communion of the almighty and holy God.

Unit 5

Walking in Divine Purpose

Spiritual Principle: My yoke is easy and my burden is light.

Chapter 13

Dealing with Betrayal

The Early Steps of Purpose

Often when people begin to walk in God's purpose for their lives drastic behavior changes occur to the point that it confuses the people around them. The confusion causes people to react toward them. Many times when people join the church after being known for living a lifestyle that conflicts with church morals, they experience distrust, ridicule, and rejection from religious people. These individuals experience ridicule from friends who have shared their previous lifestyles because of the unexpected changes in their behavior. They also experience mistrust, conflicting behavior, and advice from family members. Such interactions can cause those who are trying to walk in purpose to feel isolated, betrayed, bound, and denied.

When people are learning to walk in their purpose they often experience a feeling of not belonging—being too good for one group and not good enough for the other group. I remember my mother praying for God to deliver me from a life of fornication, and when the deliverance came and I refused to date until I found someone I felt I could marry, she thought I had gone too far and advised me to get a girlfriend before my nature went to my head. My mother's advice was given out of her love and concern for me, but what she did not understand was that the advice was also a betrayal to who I had become in God. I could no longer walk in casual fornication and fulfill God's purpose for my life.

Jesus' experiences in leaving the Garden of Gethsemane are an example for believers who are struggling with how to walk in their divine purpose. Jesus' enemies were informed of His location by Judas, one of His chosen disciples. Judas confirmed his betrayal with a kiss, which was the symbol of brotherly love and trust. Even though Judas' betrayal did not surprise Jesus, the nature in which he did it caused Jesus to ask him, "Do you betray Me with a kiss?" To choose the symbol of brotherly love and trust for his betrayal as well as reveal the special meeting place of Jesus and His disciples reveals the depths of Judas' betrayal. After Jesus' struggle to accept His destiny with the cross, He saw His capturers—men of His own people—being led by one of His chosen disciples.

The Enemy Knows Where You Are

In choosing to make the changes necessary to walk in divine destiny, it is important to understand that the enemy knows where you are. Just as Jesus was betrayed by someone close to Him, we must realize there is someone close to us that will reveal where we are to our enemy. Our betrayer is our own flesh, which does not get saved but has the same desires even when we are committed to serving God. This is the battle Paul wrote about to the Romans (Romans 7:13-25) indicating that when he would do good he found that evil was present with him. The devil knows the desires of our flesh and has access to our flesh. He uses that access to escalate those desires in an attempt to betray our spiritual natures. By being aware that our flesh is in conflict with our spirit and our desire to fulfill God's purpose, we are better prepared to deny the desires of the flesh. It is through self-denial and God's grace that we fight the warfare of the flesh and the spirit to overcome the betrayal of the flesh.

Our flesh operates much like a catcher in a baseball game. The catcher is the closest person to the batter, but he is not on the side of the batter. The catcher positions himself between the batter and the umpire and gives signals to the pitcher to strike out the batter. Our flesh is the closest thing to us. It abides between our spirit and Jesus and allows the enemy to know our weaknesses and desires.

We can operate in the assurance that, like the umpire, Jesus is positioned higher than our flesh. He is able to see the strike zone of our lives. He might allow the enemy to attempt to strike us out, but He will call the illegal pitches that come our way. However, unlike the umpire, Jesus is not neutral in the game of life; He is on our side.

Proclaiming Your Purpose in Power

In facing the crowd in Gethsemane, Jesus asked them who they were seeking, and when they said "Jesus of Nazareth" He proclaimed, "I am He." This proclamation caused the men to draw back and fall to the ground. Like Jesus, it is important for those attempting to walk in divine purpose to learn to proclaim their purpose in power. Proclamation occurs when we speak in agreement with God, and power occurs when we speak in faith. When we know what God would have us to do, we can use the assurance of the Word and the power of the Spirit to proclaim our divine purpose. Such proclamation has a threefold effect on the enemy and the people within our sphere of influence.

First, our proclamation of purpose neutralizes the influence of the enemy. When we use the power of God to make such proclamations, the shackles that the enemy has placed on our lives are shattered and the yokes of hindrance are broken. Just as the men fell to the ground when Jesus said "I am He," our rebellious and sinful natures are subdued through our testimony of God's will for our lives.

Secondly, our proclamation of purpose frees others who are within our area of influence. Just as Jesus instructed the mob to let the disciples go, we can bring deliverance and freedom to others through our proclamations. I remember being at my college homecoming football game shortly after accepting my call into ministry. My wife and I were wearing matching warm-up suits with three crosses etched across the back along with JESUS transcribed in bold letters. After the game a young man walked up to me and said thank you. When I asked him for what, he said he had watched us during the game, and the fact that we were not afraid to proclaim Jesus in that environment inspired him. He confessed that he knew God was calling him into ministry. However, he was afraid to go forward in his calling because of his age and the influence of people around him.

After talking and exchanging telephone numbers, the young man called me a couple of months later and informed me that he had preached his initial sermon. He thanked us for the inspiration and strength in our proclamations of purpose and our testimony of God's involvement in our struggles to fulfill purpose.

Our proclamations of purpose can also bring healing to others as we operate in the function of our purpose. During Jesus' arrest, He made a proclamation of action while acting as healer and deliverer. Jesus had Peter put his sword away and healed Malchus' ear, which Peter had so impulsively cut off (Luke 22:51). Our words combined with our actions of purpose can bring healing to others.

When my wife preached her first sermon, she was very shy and afraid to face the crowd. As she stood and started to speak the fear left and she began to operate in a spirit of boldness and power. At the end of the message, the wife of a pastor who was present in the congregation came forward to the altar. The lady confessed that God had called her to preach but she had been afraid to step forward. A week later we received a call from a neighbor who was also present at the event. He stated that he had answered his call into ministry because he was inspired by my wife's actions and was able to overcome his own uncertainties. When walking in divine purpose, it is important to make proclamations of word and demonstrations of actions that agree with the Word of God. Doing so will transform us and the people within our sphere of influence.

Chapter 14

Operating in a Bound Condition

Bound by Love

As Jesus was preparing to leave the Garden of Gethsemane, He was bound and led to the dwelling of the high priest. For the rest of His natural life on earth, He would be bound in one fashion or another. He would operate toward fulfillment of His purpose in a bound condition. Walking in divine purpose requires one to operate in a bound condition. Because of Jesus' demonstration of power through His proclamation, we know it was not the ropes, soldiers, nails, spikes, or tomb that bound Jesus; rather it was His love, passions, and desires. Jesus' love for His Father and humanity, His passion to fulfill the will of God for His life, and His desires to be obedient and faithful are the forces that bound Him as He left the garden and went to the cross. These same three forces are present in the lives of those who attempt to walk in divine purpose.

We were not designed to operate on our own but rather in a communal relationship with God. In this relationship, we are restricted and empowered by God's Word, Spirit, and love. In Paul's address to the Ephesians, he quoted from Psalm 68 in explaining how Jesus ascended and led captivity captive and gave gifts to mankind (Ephesians 4:8). The Old Testament prophet Hosea warns about the breaking of restraints leading to bloodshed and destruction (Hosea 4:2). The story of his wife also demonstrates how the casting off of righteous restraints can lead to our lives being restrained by unrighteous and unkind forces that use us up. As humans, we will be subject to some force outside of ourselves through our love, passion, and desires. We have been given the gift of choice and can choose to be restrained by the will of God or subject to evil forces that have unrighteous agendas.

Bound by Our Passions

As humans, we are bound by our love; therefore, it is important to love God first with our heart, soul, mind and strength. Our love is the key force that drives our passions and desires, and it is paramount that we love God. Because love is such a dominant force in our lives, we will have strong desires and passions for whatever we love. It is through our passions and desires that we often fall in love or remain in love.

When we desire something, we draw close to it and involve it in our lives or schedule our lives around it. A person who has a strong desire for basketball usually spends time learning about the game and develops a favorite team or teams. When they attend a game of their favorite team, their desire for basketball is rewarded with the things they like about the game. Often there is a desire to attend more games as this feeling of reward increases, and soon it becomes a passion. At this point, mementos of the game usually show up in the person's life and they begin to schedule a portion of their life around their favorite team. Tickets from key games are kept, jerseys, posters, cups, umbrellas, and sports regalia are often purchased with team logos on them. The more of a passion this activity becomes, the more time, money, energy, and attention it receives. This process of desire, reward, and passion creates a bond between an individual and the object of their love.

If the object of a person's love is something negative and destructive in nature, that person can easily be pulled into a dysfunctional and disruptive lifestyle. This is where evil spiritual forces will attempt to push passions into addictions. They will use the temporary reward of self-gratification that comes with desired activities and escalate them into the harmful yokes and shackles that prevent productivity and fulfillment. These spiritual forces even take harmless activities and escalate them to the point of addiction and dysfunction.

Because of the desired rewards of the gratification process, it is important to love God first and foremost (with all our heart, soul, mind, and strength). When we love God in this manner, we will desire the things of God and seek to engage with God. As we engage with God on different levels the presence and blessedness of God will be rewarding to our spirits, and we will develop a passion for God and the things of God. We will begin to schedule our lives around God and make available our energy, money, and talents for the service of God.

When God is the object of our love, He protects us from the spiritual forces that attempt to escalate the other passions in our lives out of control. In this process, it is important to understand that there is not a secular world and a religious world. God proclaimed, "The earth is the Lord's and everything in it, the world and all who live in it." When we attempt to make secular worlds, we tell God that He is not invited into the activities of our world. This attempt diminishes our ability to activate the power and protection of God in our lives because God does not dwell where He is not honored.

Bound to Honor God

In America, we are suffering from the humanistic delusion of trying to live in a secular world. We forget that the earth and all of its fullness belongs to the Lord (Psalm 24:1). We also misquote the Constitution of the United States in this effort. It says "separation of church and state," not separation of God and state. We fail to deal with the differences of the two statements. America developed into a world power not because of our goodness but because we honored God as a nation, and as we have refused to honor Him as a nation we have declined. In whatever we attempt to separate from God, we allow ourselves to stop giving Him the honor He desires and we become subject to spiritual forces of evil that would disrupt our productivity and fulfillment to the glory of God. For this reason we must invite God into all activities of our lives. Remember, don't leave home without Him, and you surely can't get home without Him.

When we do all that we do in the presence of God and for His glory, we bond ourselves to God and the fulfillment of His purpose. If we are not bound to our purpose in God then we will become distracted by the forces around us. This bonding fills us with the things of God and prevents us from having empty spaces for evil to occupy and taint. Being bound to God frees us from the control of evil forces and minimizes their influence on our lives. In our bonding with God, our passions become more righteous and productive in the fulfillment of our lives and the will of God.

When we choose to walk in divine purpose, we must be ready to operate in a bound condition for the remainder of our natural lives. Fulfillment of divine purpose is a lifelong commitment for all believers. Our faithfulness to that commitment enables our desire for the things of God to keep us from being distracted, deterred, and destroyed by negative non-productive forces. Our desire of fulfillment also keeps a balance with the positive desires and passions that we develop in life. Because we are bonded to God, our desires and passions will be for the things of God, and that bonding will enable us to endure the temptations of our flesh and the distractions of the enemy. Like Jesus we must allow our love for God and His people to drive our desires and passions in life.

Facing Denial

Our commitment to fulfilling God's purpose for our lives prepares us as vessels through which God delivers prophecies into the lives of others. Jesus delivered similar prophecies into the life of Peter during the greatest failure in his life. As Jesus left the Garden of Gethsemane, He faced denial by His chief spokesperson. Three times Peter denied that he knew the Lord or that he was one of Jesus' disciples. This denial was driven by Peter's fear for his own life. Peter denied knowing Jesus, being with Jesus, and being a disciple of Jesus. While this denial and rejection occurred, Jesus looked at Peter and delivered prophecy into his life. When Jesus looked at Peter it caused him to remember the word of prophecy that was spoken earlier about his denial.

Peter's act of denial is symbolic of the rejection and denial that people walking in purpose often experience from family members and loved ones. The act of walking in purpose can cause such a dynamic change in a person's life that people close to them have trouble understanding who they really are or what motivates their actions. This happens because God requires behavior that doesn't always make sense to our natural way of life. Often in the fulfillment of purpose, people walk away from successful careers to do work that doesn't pay much or might not be understood for its value by others. Because others are not bound by your commitment to the Lord, they might not understand your actions. However, it is important to understand the importance and value of your walk of purpose and not allow yourself to be swayed by the reactions of people close to you.

When facing denial and rejection by people close to you, it is important to hear the voice of God through His Word, through His Spirit, and through His love that allows Him to speak confirmation through the words and actions of others. Fulfilling God's purpose for my own life required me to give up a career that was successful and rewarding. When I gave up that career to do the work of ministry that God had for my life, I was ridiculed by some people close to me. They felt I was making a mistake because my career was successful and helpful to others. At that point, it was important for me to know what God was saying to me and to trust Him to take care of my needs and bring rewards into my life while I fulfilled His purpose. It may not make sense in the natural to you as well. This is where we must walk by faith and not by sight. Now as I look back at my sacrifice, I am aware of how God blessed me and took care of my family while doing the ministry work He assigned to me.

When I met my wife, I knew she was the one for my life on the first day that we met. Within three months we were married, and this upset her family because they did not even know me and thought she was making a big mistake. The two of us knew that God was leading us in the relationship and had brought us together for His purpose. It was difficult to explain this understanding to others who were not walking in our shoes. It was hard for us to understand it ourselves, but we knew in our hearts that we were doing the right thing. When my wife became concerned about her family's reaction I told her they would be all right when they saw that she was all right. We both found assurance in knowing that God had brought us together in His purpose.

Within a year's time the family got to know me and we developed wonderful relationships. Over the past twenty-four years of marriage God has allowed us to raise our children, teach school together, help many young people at key times in their lives, and also work as ministers together, blessing many individuals and families. Twenty-four years ago we had to trust in God when people did not believe our report. We had to trust in that report and deliver the prophecy that God was leading us in marriage. Many of the children we taught began to look on us as mother and father figures in their lives. Our students saw our relationship as an example of a couple walking in God's purpose together. The prophecy we spoke in saying that God was leading us in our relationship was delivered in the lives of people who saw God using us to bless others.

Expect people to react to some of the sudden shifts that occur when you begin walking in your divine purpose. You should not expect to convince them just with your words but rather allow God to convince them through your actions in Him. As the old saying goes, the proof is in the pudding. As you walk in fulfillment, God will remind people of the prophecy they see being fulfilled as He operates through your life.

Chapter 15

Trial of Testimony

Testify of the Kingdom of God

When you choose to walk in divine purpose, life often presents trials that result from your testimony of convictions. Being true to God's purpose can put you in conflict with the kingdoms of this world. Because most people choose to practice sinful ways, they are often uncomfortable around someone who is committed to living for God. Many relationships break up because one person chooses to avoid fornication while their partner is comfortable having sex outside of marriage. Individuals who walk into this type of commitment often find themselves lonely because so many people take having sex outside of marriage as a casual social act.

In order to serve the kingdom of God, remember that His kingdom is not of this world. Therefore, those who are committed to establishing the kingdom of God in this world must be prepared to face resistance. Jesus was tried for His testimony of who He was because His testimony conflicted with those who had agendas of their own. The Jews were concerned with reestablishing the kingdom of Israel rather than the kingdom of God. Their expectation was for God to reestablish their kingdom with them as His favorite children. When Jesus indicated that He was more concerned with the kingdom of God, they rejected Him as their king. However, Jesus' responsibility was to testify of the kingdom of God.

As Christians we are responsible to testify in words and actions of the kingdom of God that transcend personal agendas and flesh-satisfying behavior patterns. We are expected to follow the patterns of Jesus by learning to place God's will above our own and to be prepared for rejection and misunderstanding. Our commitment to remain faithful in the face of rejections becomes a testimony of the power of God. Our convictions and presence often make people feel uncomfortable when they are in the midst of doing something contrary to God's Word.

A friend of mine once told me that she did not want to hear me talk about living for Jesus because she had plans for the weekend and was not going to change them. Her statement indicated that those plans involved actions she considered sinful, but she didn't want to be reminded of her responsibility to God. It is our testimony of word and deed that reminds people of their responsibility to God. I chose not to preach to my friend but rather just be nice and finish the project we were working on. (Later my friend told me that she had changed her mind and her plans for the weekend.) At one point I felt like I had missed an opportunity to minister to my friend in a needed time. However, God showed me that He also uses the testimony of our presence and by His power (and not our own) ministers to His people. God helped me to understand that when my friend asked me not to preach about living for Jesus, He had already used my presence and the testimony of my life to remind my friend of her responsibility to God.

Jesus demonstrated the power of presence when He died on the cross in such a manner of commitment to God that the Roman centurion involved in His crucifixion proclaimed Him to be the Son of God. This is a testimony of the power of God to move on the hearts of people through what seems like defeat. To walk in divine purpose, you must be prepared to face defeat in the eyes of this world so that God can be glorified by actions that can't be explained or don't make sense to this world. God will often set you up to fail in the eyes of this world so that He can demonstrate His power and righteousness are not of this world but beyond the limitations of world powers, desires, and beliefs.

Testify of the Power of God

As believers, remember that we are not expected to do God's job. We are expected to do His work. God's work involves the assignments He gives us so that He can get His job done through us and sometimes in spite of us. The testimony of the Roman centurion demonstrates how God works though the situations in our lives to reach people in ways that amaze us. We must be like Jesus in remaining focused on our purpose and expectations of God to glorify His kingdom. If God knows that He can receive glory through us He will allow us to use His glory to exalt the kingdom of God.

The centurion experienced the glory of God through the death of Jesus on the cross. Jesus' work was to die at the hands of the Romans by the request of the Jewish religious leaders. God's job was to save the world through Jesus' fulfilling the law with His death and inspiring the Romans to become the chief spreaders of the gospel throughout the world. The testimony that Jesus gave in His death inspired the Roman centurion and indicates that God allowed Jesus, the Son of Man, to use His glory to begin the process of inspiring the Romans. This is also demonstrated in the interactions between Jesus and Pilate during Jesus' trial. Both Pilate and his wife were inspired by their interactions with Jesus. God was already working on the Romans through the trial and death of Jesus.

The trial and death of Jesus led to the personal testimonies of three very influential Romans about the righteousness of Jesus. Pilate, his wife, and the centurion were all inspired through Jesus' public defeat, which led to some of the most influential testimonies of the kingdom of God. Because Jesus remained focused on His work, God allowed Him to use the glory of God so that He could do His work of saving the world and inspiring the Romans to carry the gospel. We must remember that God is always up to more than we see in the circumstances around us. God will allow us to undergo experiences that have both natural and spiritual implications for our lives and the kingdom of God. Our trials become God's avenue of testimonies for those who need to experience the glory of God in action. Our trials also put events into action that are important to God's master plan.

As Jesus was being tried by Pilate, He testified of the power of His Father. We are sometimes placed in events that demonstrate the power of God to deliver in difficult situations. God demonstrated His power to the world through the suffering of Jesus on the cross. God demonstrates His power to discourage the enemies of creation from trying to prevent His will and to encourage the righteous to trust Him. We must understand that God's kingdom is not of this world, and He will use events of tragedy and suffering to demonstrate His power to enable us to overcome.

About fifteen years ago I was pastoring a church in my hometown when a church member's son was shot and killed. I worked with the family all week, encouraging them and reminding them that God would see them through the situation. On Friday night (the night before the funeral) my brother was killed in an automobile accident. He was driving my car when a drunk driver ran into him. My brother died at the scene of the accident, and my brother-in-law's girlfriend was placed in critical condition. After informing my family and consoling my mother and sisters, I went home crying. My wife was a major help to me at a time when my peace left me and I felt broken and hurt.

When I made the decision to call a friend in the ministry to preach the funeral of the young man, God spoke to me and said, "You are about to mess up." I told God I could not preach a funeral in my condition. God said to me, "Now that there is a little trouble in your home are you going to bail out on My people? You have been telling them all week that I'll make a way and see them through. Now you don't have to tell them, you can show them, because now they know that you understand how they feel. If they see you stand there tomorrow they will know that I'll make a way."

The next day I was still crying when I headed to the family house. All I could do was be obedient and trust in God. When I arrived at the house the young man's mother came out and ran across the road to meet me. At that moment my tears stopped and dried up. I met the family with encouragement of the power and love of God. As I was preaching the eulogy I kept thinking about my brother. Both bodies were handled by the same funeral home, and in the middle of the message my strength gave way and I felt my knees buckle. As I was waiting to fall I felt what seemed to be a large hand holding me in the middle of my back, but I saw no one. For the remainder of the message, that hand held me even when my strength had given way. God said to me, "I did not bring you up here to fall; I just wanted them to know that I would make a way." Someone who knew about my brother's death said after the message, "My God, what a strong man." I said, "No, I have a strong God."

Through these events, God also let me know that He will make a way beyond the abilities of my humanity. He allowed me to be a part of His demonstration of power and love for His people in difficult situations.

Testify of the Righteousness of God

As Jesus was being tried by Pilate, He also testified of the righteousness of God. Jesus understood that His Father was requiring something of Him that He did not want to experience and that it would cause Him to suffer. However, Jesus did not rebel against God's judgment; rather He testified of God's right to require His suffering. Jesus realized that God's requirements of His earthly life were authorized by the Father's sovereignty and motivated by His love for humanity. Believers must understand that God is the righteous judge of all creation because He is the Creator and sustainer of all that exists. God's judgments and His actions are always motivated by His love for creation.

Empowered by the understanding of God's authority and love, we are better prepared to suffer through our human experience for the glory of God. What God requires of us is needed for the testimony of the kingdom of God, and our obedience becomes a wonderful testimony of the power of God in the lives of humanity. We become living testimonies of the power and love of God that inspires other people in our influence.

Unit 6

Fulfilling Divine Purpose

Spiritual Principle: Do all things as if you do them for the Lord.

Chapter 16

Surrendering Your Being to God

Being Open to God

J esus' life as the Son of Man ends on a cross at a place called Calvary. Jesus is placed on the cross with His arms stretched wide, with only His undergarment on. He is uncovered and lifted up above the earth for the entire world to see. Jesus is placed in an open and vulnerable position, which illustrates the need to be open to the will of God for our lives. Jesus' openness and vulnerability became a testimony that affected those who were around Him. During the crucifixion, Jesus got the attention of believers and non-believers alike.

Jesus gave Himself to the kingdom of God as a sacrifice for creation. His body was broken so that we might be made whole, His blood was shed to atone for our sins, and His life was given so that we might have life eternal. Isaiah prophesied of Jesus' sacrifice in the fifty-third chapter of his book of prophecies. Jesus faced an open shame so that humanity would not be put to spiritual shame (Galatians 3:13-14).

Just as Jesus was willing to submit to the will of God and be open to God's purpose for His life, even to death on the cross (Philippians 2:5-8), we must be open to God's will for our lives, even when our flesh does not desire God's will. Jesus had to struggle with His flesh in the garden and put it under subjection to God's purpose through prayer and obedience (Matthew 26:36-46). Through our prayer life, we can become obedient to God's Word and will for our lives. Like Jesus, we are strengthened in our prayer time with God, and our flesh is placed under subjection so that we can fulfill purpose.

After Jesus left the Garden of Gethsemane even His enemies assisted in His fulfillment of God's will for His life. They placed His human nature in a state of subjection, openness, vulnerability, brokenness, and death, thereby freeing His divine nature to fulfill His purpose. When our human nature is placed in subjection our divine nature is being freed to operate in obedience to God's will. Like Jesus we must experience a state of openness to God and with humanity. We have to come to the point where we discard our social, emotional, and spiritual masks that we often show to the world. With these masks we hide our feelings of pain, doubt, and at times joy so that we can present only those feelings we wish to express. Much like actors on a stage, we often go through life following the script we think will cause people to applaud and reward us. In removing the masks we become accessible to God and to people who need to experience God through us. Our openness allows us to be receptive to the will of God for our lives and honest with ourselves and others about those experiences. Jesus did not go to the cross acting like Superman; rather He allowed His brokenness to show.

Being Vulnerable to God

One of the reasons we hide and avoid being open is because when we become open to God and others, we are vulnerable. This is a condition we avoid because it makes us feel weak and look helpless. At the crucifixion people in the crowd said that Jesus could save others but He could not save Himself. Vulnerability is not a weakness in God but rather a strength. This is often difficult to understand because vulnerabilities in our natural existence can make us subject to demonic forces. However, in our subjection to the Spirit of God we become vulnerable to Him and to His will.

You cannot love without being vulnerable, just as God is vulnerable to us through His love. God is the most powerful being in existence, able to do anything. Yet He was willing to move heaven and earth to save man after Adam broke His heart in the garden.

The Bible says God grieved over making man when He saw him in such a sinful condition. But God the Word was willing to leave heaven and give up most of His glory for about thirty-three years to save this same sinful man. God was willing to become man, who was vulnerable to criticism, rejection, and even death. On the cross Jesus showed His vulnerability to humanity through His suffering. He even asked His Father to forgive humanity for the acts they were doing to Him. To our natural senses, it appears that Jesus was weak, much like we say that people in love are weak when someone is doing them wrong, yet they keep on loving them.

When we are in love with someone we become vulnerable to that person. We even call it "falling" in love, which indicates a state of vulnerability. Being in love with my wife causes me to want to be with her, miss her when she is not there, and gives me a sense of not being complete when she is not near. My love for my wife causes feelings that I don't have for other women. These feelings cause me to feel emotions of jealousy in relationship to my wife. However, the feelings for my wife are helpful to me when I see another woman that I feel is beautiful. The love I have for my wife and the willingness to please God gives me the strength not to be vulnerable to the lures of other women.

It is in our vulnerabilities to God's will that we are able to receive the strength of God. The Bible says that we are made strong in our weakness. This scripture indicates that when we take on the nature of God and become vulnerable to His will, we have access to His power. Abraham had to show his vulnerability to God's will in his willingness to offer his son Isaac before he could become the father of the faithful. Elisha had to show his obedience and service to Elijah under criticism before he could receive the mantle of power from Elijah. Peter had to be willing to place his life on the line at Pentecost before he could become the spokesperson for the early church. The Bible teaches us that in seeking to save our lives we will lose them, but in our willingness to lose our lives for God's will we will save them eternally. When we become open and vulnerable to God's will, He influences situations to assist in our fulfillment of purpose (Romans 8:28).

God uses the experiences in our lives to teach us to become open and vulnerable to His will. In order to experience such vulnerability to the will of God, it is important for us to discover that we are spiritual beings in natural bodies. In discovering and understanding our true nature we are better prepared to suffer loss in the natural that we may gain in the spirit with God. This is what Jesus demonstrated on the cross and why He would not come down when asked to do so. Jesus understood that God's will involved Him losing His natural life for the spiritual lives of humanity. Jesus' act was motivated by His love for God and humanity, and this is where He was vulnerable. Therefore, His vulnerability to God and humanity gave Him power over the natural desires of His human existence. Like Jesus our vulnerabilities in the love of God and love of people give us power over the natural desires and weaknesses of our flesh.

When our flesh is in subjection we are better prepared to walk in obedience to God's will and be broken for the good of the kingdom of God. Through our submission to God's will we are able to surrender our lives to His purpose and become a living sacrifice for the kingdom (Romans 12:1-2). God orchestrates and uses the situations in our lives to prepare us and assist us in fulfilling His purpose. These types of forces prepare us to become God's example to the world. God uses us and situations to demonstrate His love and power to heal, deliver, and transform through adversity. We face persecution, sickness, disappointment, and even open shame so that the world knows that God is able to deliver and sustain.

I remember being assigned as principal to a school that had some of the lowest test scores in the state. This was the first year the state decided to print the scores of schools on the failure list. People asked why I was assigned to this school and felt that it was a bad assignment. During my first year a reporter showed up at the school to do an article on why the students performed so poorly on their tests. The article exposed our weaknesses to the general public and did not reflect favorably on us as an institution of education. I had to answer questions about our school from people who read the article. I also had to speak encouragement to the students, parents, and staff to keep believing in our school. This task was frustrating because it presented me as the leader of a school that was failing. I had to accept the label even when I was not comfortable with it.

My acceptance of the label allowed me not to accept the premise that things were all right and should remain the same. When the reporter came to interview me at the school, I asked a favor of him. I asked him to give me a year to work on our problems and come back and interview me again. As I promised, I was open and truthful with him in the interview, which was hurtful to read, but God used it to help us. One year later we had some of the best test scores in the county and our students, staff, and parents felt good about the success God had given us through commitment, hard work, and trust in Him. Through my willingness to be put in what seemed like a shameful situation, God was able to use me to be a blessing to so many people. God will use us as examples of His love and power to deliver if we trust and obey Him.

Experiencing Brokenness

The writer of Psalm 119 declares that it was good that he be afflicted in order to learn God's law. New Testament writing informs us that Jesus comforts us in our tribulations so that we are able to comfort others in their times of trouble (1 Corinthians 1:3-7). Jesus also experienced brokenness during His journey to the cross, and through His brokenness we are made whole. His body was broken by the hands of men and His spirit was broken by the knowledge of being separated from His Father. Even His relationship with His Father was broken by the sins of the world to the point that He felt forsaken. However, Jesus was able to endure brokenness, and therefore He and those who believe in Him are made stronger because of it.

Brokenness is the awareness and acceptance of our lack of wholeness and continuous being. Brokenness makes us aware of our lack of sufficiency and our need for God's interventions in our lives. We experience different levels of brokenness at different times in our lives. These experiences can be cumulative in nature throughout the course of our lives and become a valuable source of information about ourselves and God's love for us. We can become cracked in which all the pieces are connected but there is a disruption in our relationships. In the cracked state we maintain the same capacity, but we become fragile because of the disruption in our relationships. We maintain a sense of functionality under limited situations, but we experience a sense of loss in value. We can also become chipped, which indicates something is missing in our relationships. When we are chipped we have a loss of capacity, and where the chipping occurs determines how much loss there is. When we become chipped we experience a sense of loss of value and functionality. We can also become shattered, which causes us to feel disjointed and disconnected. When shattered we lose all our capacity because of our lack of connectivity. In this state we experience a sense of loss of value, functionality, and purpose.

Three main causes of brokenness can be identified as being knocked down, dropped, or falling down. Sometimes we are knocked down, which involves hurt caused by the callous actions of others. Whether we are knocked down accidentally or intentionally, both of them cause hurt and disruptions in our sense of being. When we are dropped it involves our misguided trust in others who let us down when we needed them and depended on them. Falling down involves the hurt inflicted upon us by our own actions. All of these methods of brokenness can be caused by accidental or intentional actions, even those which are self-inflicted.

As believers and followers of Jesus Christ we experience brokenness that results from our actions, the actions of others against us, and sometimes by the circumstances of life. God uses the brokenness in our lives to shape our spiritual character and transform us to overcome natural weaknesses. In our brokenness we often reflect on life more from a spiritual perspective, and we discover what is really important. We also give God more attention during our times of brokenness, and He is able to impart more spiritual knowledge and strength within us. The Scriptures teach that because of our suffering for the righteousness of Christ we shall be glorified with Christ (Romans 8:17).

Through our openness, vulnerability, and brokenness for God, He is able to place our human nature in subjection until it dies to the things that hinder and separate us from our divine purpose. The more our human nature dies to sinful desires, the more our divine nature is freed to empower us to do God's will and fulfill His purpose. Just as our human nature desires the things of this world, our divine nature desires the things of God. It is through our divine nature that we discover our spiritual identities as children of God and understand what we are given to fulfill God's purpose for our lives.

Chapter 17

Moving Under Grace

Influencing People to Move Under Grace

On the cross, Jesus became the center of attraction to His friends and enemies. People were drawn to the cross for different reasons, and He influenced those who noticed more than a man dying on a tree. One of the thieves crucified with Jesus stopped railing against Him and asked Jesus to remember him in the kingdom. This confession and request indicated that the thief began to see the divine nature of Jesus because he asked to be remembered in the kingdom to come. Somehow he understood and believed that Jesus' death on the cross would not be the end of Jesus but rather free Him to be in authority of the souls of humanity.

The presence of Jesus on the cross influenced the thief to move under grace. The thief did not ask to be excused of his sins; rather he expected Jesus to have the power to move him beyond those sins. God's job as indicated in John 3:16 was being fulfilled in Jesus while He was on the cross. Even before His death He was completing His work of drawing people unto Himself (John 12:32). Jesus' response to the thief gave him assurance that Jesus was able and willing to accept people who are drawn to Him no matter the circumstances of their lives.

As disciples of Christ, we are able to influence the lives of people we interact with. God uses us as instruments or presenters of grace in which He completes His job in Jesus to save creation. We face the struggles of life and allow God to enable us to overcome them. Through our situations people experience Christ operating in our lives, and they are drawn to grace. God allows us to be placed in situations so that He can influence others through His interventions in our lives. We are not the givers of grace but rather conduits through which Christ can be experienced by unbelievers. The greatest message that can be shared through disciples is to experience Christ just as the lame man looked on Peter and John and was lifted up in power to overcome his human condition, which prevented him from allowing God to work on his spiritual condition.

Influencing Others to Resist Unrighteousness

The experiences that people have with Jesus through our testimony of words, deeds, and presence will lead them to resist unrighteousness, accept their sins, and ask for God's forgiveness. On the cross Jesus influenced the thief through His words, actions, and presence to rebuke the unrighteousness that He saw in the other thief. The thief did not acknowledge the unrighteousness in himself and the other thief until he shifted his focus from himself and his situation to Jesus. When he focused on Jesus he began to rebuke the other man for his acts of unrighteousness. Like Jesus, we can influence people to resist unrighteousness through our words, actions, and presence. The resistance that comes through our influence could transform the words and actions of those we influence.

When we shift our focus to Jesus in the fulfillment of God's will for our lives, we are better able to acknowledge our faults and the faults of others. It is important for the people we influence to witness our commitment to righteousness. I remember after I answered my call into ministry I was at my college Homecoming celebration when my friends from college wanted to go for a ride. As we got in the van and headed out, the first stop was at a convenience store to purchase beer. I asked those who were going into the store to bring me a six-pack of Coke, and everyone smiled. As we rode and talked, they drank beer and I drank Coke.

The driver went to a club that was one of our favorite places before I started preaching. We parked in front of the club and I told them I was staying in the van to talk to people outside. My friends began to notice that as young ladies came to the van my focus was on them as people rather than as opportunities of conquest. Even when guys stopped by the van we talked about where people were in life and the fulfillment of their lives. Our conversation in this type of setting usually focused on outward pleasures, but it seemed to have shifted to inward concerns and a focus of purpose. We sat there for more than two hours and no one got out of the van. I had never seen my friends react to going into a club this way before. My actions of conviction for my calling to God had an influence on their actions. I did not ask them not to go into the club, and I am not saying that going into the club would have been sinful. I am saying that I knew it was not the place for me anymore, and I acted on that commitment and it influenced my friends. They made a powerful statement by not going into the club that night, and most of those friends are now preaching. We all knew from our past experiences that the club represented an opportunity to engage in sinful activities.

God can influence people through us when we allow Him to move our human nature out of the way so that people can see the divine nature of Jesus through our words, actions, and presence. Through the crucifixion of our fleshly desires, God can fulfill His purpose in us by influencing people to move under grace. Through the crucifixion of our fleshly desires we become aware of and embrace the divine nature that exists within us.

Influencing People to Speak Life

When our divine nature comes forward we operate as living spirits (speaking spirits) that were created in the image and likeness of God. As speaking spirits we have the ability to speak things into existence. God's ability to speak things into being is illustrated in Genesis 1-2 as He releases such things as light, the firmament, waters, vegetation, and lights in the firmament (Genesis 1:1-14). In the process of creating humanity God shared His creative ability with humanity; therefore we are able to speak things into existence in agreement with God's Word (1 John 2:5), God's will (1 John 5:14-15), and God's love (1 John 3:1-3).

The Bible instructs believers that the power of life and death are in our tongues (Proverbs 18:21). As a young child my mother spoke vision into my life that helped me to focus on life. My mother convinced me to go to college before I started school. Before I knew what it was I told people I was going to college to be a schoolteacher. After my mother spoke the vision into me I began to speak it myself, and as I grew in knowledge and understanding the vision she spoke into me helped me to stay focused on expectations for my life.

As living spirits who are able to speak things into existence we must remain holy so that we can speak holy and living things into existence. The taint of unrighteousness and sin can cause us to speak cursed things or death into existence. When we share our existence of life with sin it attempts to become a part of us to fill our soul and rule over us (Genesis 4:7). Sin attempts to influence our thoughts, desires, actions, and words and thereby whatever we release into the natural world in which we live. Such influence can cause us to speak from a tainted heart unrighteous words that bring darkness and death in our lives and the lives of others.

People who are trapped in sinful lifestyles often speak dead things to one another and encourage the continuation of dead acts. Many of the people around Jesus' cross tried to speak dead things into Him, but His divine nature would not accept the words of death and selfish desire. The divine nature of Jesus allowed Him to move beyond the words of the crowd and speak life into those who could hear Him. Not everyone will hear our words of life, but those who have an ear (spiritual awareness) will hear and be influenced by our words of life. Both of the thieves were trapped in sinful lifestyles that caused them to be bound at the end of their earthly existence. Even through their sinful lifestyles God allowed them to be placed in a situation where they could experience the saving presence of Jesus. Both thieves were offered the same grace by being placed in the presence of Jesus, but only one of them received the invitation of life.

The sinful influence attempts to spread through the continuum of life that exists between humanity and God. God will not allow sin to abide in His continuum. Therefore, He separates the taint of sin from His presence in an act to minimize its influence on humanity.

We must remember that the devil could not bring sin and death into the existence of humanity; he had to deceive humanity with words of death that influenced them to disobey God (Genesis 3:1-7). The influence of his words of death caused humanity to be separated from the presence of God. It was at this time of separation that the Flaming Sword came forward from God to keep the cursed things from the tree of life. The sword enabled the angel to fulfill God's purpose of keeping the cursed things from the continuum of life. Jesus' words on the cross separated the thief from the cursed things and brought him into paradise with Jesus.

Because we are living speaking spirits, we have the ability to release life, holiness, and the blessings of God into the natural world. Not only can we speak deliverance into our lives, but also into the lives of others. While Jesus was on the cross He spoke the blessings of God into the life of the thief. Jesus' presence even caused the thief to speak life as he rebuked his friend for railing against Jesus, and he began to speak of the kingdom of God. Many times our position is not to release people from their conditions but rather to speak of God's deliverance through their conditions. Jesus did not move to release the thief from the cross; rather He spoke of His deliverance through death on the cross. Sometimes people are placed into conditions as part of God's way of transforming their spiritual lives to serve as living witnesses of His power to sustain in difficult times and situations.

I once viewed a movie about a man who was seeking Jesus after His crucifixion. I remember a scene about a woman who was blind and met Jesus while He was on earth. The woman remained blind after meeting Jesus and later met a man who was seeking the Jesus he had heard so much about. He had met people who had been healed by Jesus of different conditions. As the woman offered the man some bread he noticed her cheerful attitude and disposition. He asked her if she knew of the man called Jesus and she said yes and that she had met Him. The man was puzzled and asked why Jesus had not healed her. The woman smiled and said that Jesus did heal her when He took away her bitterness about her condition of life. She explained that meeting Jesus enabled her to see her condition through her divine nature. In doing so she discovered that God had purpose for her in her condition. She realized that God could use her to show people how they are blessed in difficult situations.

The man's encounter with the woman helped to open his eyes of spiritual blindness that kept him from seeing the spiritual Jesus that existed in all the children of God. The man had been seeking the natural Jesus and was disappointed that he did not get to talk with Him. However, through his experiences with those he contacted he realized he was able to experience Jesus through those who were touched by Him. The man's experience with the woman caused him to reflect on all the people he had encountered, and thus he connected the message of Jesus' love and presence in the lives of His believers.

God allows us to release blessing into the lives of others through the prophetic utterance of the Holy Spirit. God has always used the prophetic utterance to reveal and release His blessings, judgments, and will into the human existence (Genesis 3:15). The prophetic utterance can release the promises that God has for our lives and prepare us for divine purpose. There are some things that will not be released in our lives until someone prophesies them to us. Prophecy activates the blessings of God that exist within us and instructs us how to use them according to His purpose for our lives. The word of God that we receive interacts with the Holy Spirit within us to activate the prophetic utterance into the lives of those we influence.

To bless the kingdom of God we must learn to work the Word of God. Oftentimes we struggle with the forces of evil in our natural abilities, laboring with the things that hinder us in life. We must allow the Holy Spirit to remind us that we are speaking spirits and designed to use the Word of God as a creative, renewing, and transforming force in our lives and the lives of those we influence. In creating the world God spoke the Word, He worked the Word. Therefore, we must learn to work the Word in our lives rather than attempt to wrestle with flesh and blood. Even when it was necessary for God to labor in this natural existence, it was the Word that became flesh and labored with us in this world. While God has assigned us to labor and toil in this world, He expects us to use the Word to empower our natural existence with the supernatural power of creation (John 14:23; Romans 10:8).

By using the Word of God in our natural existence we are able to apply the knowledge, wisdom, understanding, and power of God to situations in our lives. When we work the Word of God through speech by faith in Christ Jesus, and in the love of God, we are able to activate the abundant life that Jesus promised to us. The natural forces of this world and the supernatural forces of creation (righteous or evil) respects and submits to the Word of God. As Jesus used the Word in His struggles with Satan, we must use the Word of God in the fulfillment of His will for our lives (Matthew 4:1-11).

Chapter 18

Finishing the Work

Embracing Forgiveness

One of the last words of Jesus on the cross was "It is finished" (John 19:30). Shortly after this happened, He bowed His head and gave up His spirit into the Father's hand. In making this statement, Jesus informed us that it is important to finish our work that is related to the divine purpose of our lives. It is not enough to talk about what we are to do; we have to get it done. Some of it might not be easy and some of it may be frightening, but we have to remove the excuses and do as the Nike people say: "Just do it!" Jesus understood what the prophets had spoken about Him. He knew what His Father required of Him, and He understood what needs creation had of Him. With such knowledge, Jesus understood what He had to do, and He was willing to give of Himself to get it done.

Jesus was willing to forgive His accusers, His betrayers, His tormentors, His unbelieving blasphemers, His murderers, and His sinful brothers and sisters. Before His death, Jesus asked His Father to "forgive them for they do not know what they are doing" (Luke 23:34). Jesus understood that He was dying for all of us and His death was necessary to redeem us from our sins. When God shows us our purpose and we are empowered to fulfill that purpose, we must be willing to give of ourselves to complete the work assigned to us. It is usually not the losing of our lives that God requires of us, but rather the giving of our lives to the fulfillment of God's purpose as a living sacrifice (Romans 12:1-2). As living sacrifices, we must be willing to forgive those who trespass against us and try to make things difficult for us.

In being able to forgive others, it is important to understand that they really don't know what they are doing. Oftentimes they understand that they are betraying you or trying to harm you, but they don't understand that they are hurting themselves more than you and that God will only allow them to go so far with their unrighteous attacks toward you. Forgiveness is necessary because the work must be done without malice. As disciples we must exemplify the forgiving nature of God. This is why the human nature must be put into subjection to fulfill purpose, because the work is completed through the divine nature. Both Jesus and Stephen (the first martyr of the church) exemplified the need for forgiveness in completing their work and expressed the divine nature operating within them (Luke 23:34; Acts 7:57-60).

Serving From an Elevated Prospective

When we learn to operate in forgiveness, then we are better prepared to look out for others. As Jesus was dying on the cross He looked down on the people around the cross and asked His Father to forgive them (Luke 23:34). Jesus also asked His beloved disciple John to take care of His earthly mother (John 19:25-27). As instruments of God we must be concerned for others and allow God to use us to bless them. God uses our afflictions to place us above the natural conditions that the people we are to help are experiencing. This allows us to look at their situation more from God's perspective rather from a human perspective. Our elevated perspectives are not to be mixed with a spirit of pride or self-glory; rather we must operate in a spirit of thanksgiving and humility. It is important to remember that our perspective has been elevated only by the grace and love of God.

I remember being falsely accused of actions that could have caused me serious complications in my ministry. I was angry and wanted to strike back at the person who made the false accusations. The incident caused me to seek God in prayer, and the Spirit of the

Lord instructed me to humble myself and not retaliate. While the situation was ongoing the person who made the accusations was placed in a condition in which they needed help. God had me positioned to assist them in their time of need, but my flesh did not want to help them. However, because I was praying God enabled me to see that the situation was not about me and my anger. Because of how God elevated my perspective I was able to put my feelings aside and help the person in need. Rather than seeing my false accuser I saw God's child in need and myself in a position to help. I was also able to see that our personal fight could hurt people that we influenced.

Though the situation brought unwanted attention it caused people who could help my ministry to see me in a positive manner because of how God used me. God even allowed the person who brought the false accusation to see the truth in the matter, and they began to view me as a person who could help them. As a result of the incident we formed a stronger relationship and were able to work together and help a lot of people.

From our elevated perspectives we are better able to see beyond the natural hindrances that keep us from seeing the whole picture. For example, when you see a rainbow it appears to be a quarter-circle or half-circle. However, if you are in a spaceship and look down on the earth you will see that a rainbow is a complete circle. In order to see the entire shape of the rainbow you have to be elevated above the earth so that the natural curvature of the earth does not block your vision. We must be elevated above our natural conditions so that our spiritual vision is not restricted. From this perspective we are able to help people to see that the answers are higher than we are. This is why the Scripture informs us to look to the hills, from whence our help comes (Psalm 121:1-2). When we elevate our perspective so that we can see more of what God is up to in our situations, we will discover our answers and our deliverance.

Surrendering Your Life to God

Jesus was required to lose His natural life as a sacrifice for all of creation, and we are asked to surrender our natural lives into God's hands as a living sacrifice. In giving our lives to God, we allow Him to put our human nature in subjection and place us in situations that allow the divine nature to be expressed and influence an unbelieving world. Our work requires us to give ourselves to Him, and God will complete His job with what we give Him. We have to overcome the fear of death in giving ourselves because God allows the "old man" (our sinful nature) to die as we give ourselves to the will of God. Our mind often rejects the notion of death because we see it as a loss, but our spiritual nature realizes that the sinful things were not ours in the first place. In putting the sinful things in our lives to death we are released from the false assignments, harmful distractions, and destiny-stealing shackles that the enemy has placed in our lives.

The last thing the natural Jesus did on the cross was to give His spirit to God. As we surrender to God we must allow the old man to die. This transformation binds us to the will of God and frees us from old sinful habits, fearful ways, and cursed attitudes that hinder our fulfillment of purpose. Once we are bound to God our divine nature is free to operate in our lives. Our divine nature allows us to operate in the presence of God and have access to the divine inspirations, transformations, and empowerments that God shares to fulfill His purpose in our lives, and for the kingdom of God.

It was when Jesus died that He fully operated in the power of God to fulfill His purpose. At death His spirit was released to operate in other realms of existence to redeem those who came before He was born in Bethlehem. At His resurrection the saints came out of their graves and appeared to others. Jesus demonstrated the power to release others through His resurrection into the divine nature. After His resurrection Jesus often demonstrated the power of His divine nature over the natural laws of existence. When appearing to His disciples He still had the wounds in His body without harm or pain, and He entered the room without opening the door (John 20:19-20). The Jews who always seemed to find Jesus and badger Him did not show up after the resurrection, and gravity could not prevent Him from going up into a cloud.

When we allow the old sinful nature to die, God resurrects us into new creatures who are better equipped to follow the divine nature. As new creatures we are able to overcome the natural tendencies of our flesh and avoid the sinful lifestyles of our past. We learn to operate from our spiritual existence more than the natural and remove some of the limitations of our fleshly existence. In examining the death of Jesus, we realize that it was not His end but rather the end of His limited existence and freed Him to return to being God. Jesus remained on earth for forty days after His resurrection, demonstrating His power over natural existence and instructing His disciples to believe and follow His examples. Like Jesus we are able to operate as overcomers and inspire others to do the same. There is a song that speaks of letting our little light shine because there might be someone in the valley trying to get home; this song reflects our new nature and purpose in God.

We are not free of our natural tendencies while we are in the flesh, but we are given the power and inspiration to overcome them to the fulfillment of God's will. From this position we are able to complete our work for God. We are also able to reach more people through our influence, much like Jesus after giving up His spirit to God. The Holy Spirit directs and assists us in completing the work that God has assigned to our lives.

Unit 7

Testimony of Divine Purpose

Spiritual Principle: We overcome in Jesus by the word of our testimony.

Chapter 19

Experiencing the Resurrection

The resurrection of Jesus is the living testimony of the fulfillment of divine purpose. The resurrection is the chief cornerstone of the Christian faith and the power that ensures believers live with God beyond the human experience. This power also assures us that we can separate from sinful bondages in the renewal of life experienced through Jesus Christ. This is where believers experience life as new creatures in the full activation of the Flaming Sword. In order to walk in this new reality of life believers must experience the resurrection, express the resurrection, and exemplify the resurrection (Philippians 3:7-11).

Exposure to the Resurrection

To experience the resurrection power of Jesus Christ you must be exposed to it, which allows you to become knowledgeable of the resurrection. Such knowledge comes through observation or communication. Since the event occurred about two thousand years ago we experience it through the communication of others (Romans 10:14-15). Through the sharing of the gospel we are able to experience the resurrection. The gospel is shared in every form of communication known to humanity and all around the world. The Holy Spirit is active in the life of the church to bear witness to the truth about Jesus the Christ, the redemptive nature of His death, and the transformational power of His resurrection.

As we accept the gospel message as truth, we become involved in the resurrection. This occurs when we believe and our faith takes us from being a spectator to being involved in the event. An old hymn asks the question "were you there when they crucified my Savior and when they nailed him to the tree?", your answer should be yes, because you believe that He took your sins to the cross thus making you a participant in His crucifixion whereby you also became a participant in His resurrection (and yours) early that Sunday morning. Those who died with Him also rose with Him to be reconciled with God the Father in the dispensation of grace. While your involvement in the crucifixion is an unpleasant thought, it is necessary to be involved in the glorious renewal of life and the power of God in humanity through the resurrection of Jesus Christ. Remember, there is no resurrection without a death.

Belief in the Resurrection

Once we are exposed to the knowledge of the resurrection we must become believers of its actuality and power. We cannot be like King Agrippa who was *almost* persuaded to believe in Jesus Christ. We must be convinced and willing to act on our convictions of the saving power of God. When we believe to the level that it changes our lives we become disciples of Christ. As disciples we are better equipped to fulfill the will of God for our lives and for the kingdom of God. God instructs us through the Word not to harden our heart when we hear it, which focuses on the good news of His salvation plan (Hebrews 3:7-11). Therefore, we must believe that God's resurrection power has the ability to transform our natures and our lives.

This is where we use the key of faith to unlock the power of God to believe beyond sight. When there was nothing God believed that there was and spoke a world into existence. Through our relationship with Christ we are able to believe in the resurrection power of God operating in our lives. We are able to know the power of His resurrection did not end when He rose but was in the early stages. We also become aware that through Christ God's resurrection power draws all of us to be reconciled with God.

It is our faith that allows us to experience the resurrection power of Christ, who rose for all of creation willing to be with God. Our belief becomes faith when we are able to believe beyond sight. In knowing that we were there at Calvary and our sins were purged, we understand that we were with Him on resurrection morning and when He declared that all authority was given unto him in heaven and earth. By our faith in this resurrection power of Christ we become the righteousness of God.

Transformed Through the Resurrection

Our belief in Christ causes us to be affected by the resurrection so much that we experience it in every part of our existence. Our experience of the resurrection causes us to obtain the power to become children of God (John 1:12). Through the resurrection of Christ, we are cleansed of our sin and brought back to life and in a right relationship with God. As children we are given authority in the kingdom of God. God also uses resurrection power to allow us to fulfill our obligation to become new creations in Christ Jesus (2 Corinthians 5:17-21). We are transformed from creatures of darkness and weakness to creations of light and power in God. We are transformed to be the children of God and moved closer to the original design to be just like Him (1 John 3:1-3).

Through our faith in Jesus Christ God gives us to power to become the children of God. As children we receive the power to walk in purpose as witnesses for Christ in our thoughts, words, and actions. We have the power to emulate the holiness of God in our lives in ways that influence others. This type of power allows us to fulfill our purpose of representing God in the land of the living. We become extensions of the presence, power, and prosperity of God that transforms the world around us.

As children of God, we become heirs of God and joint-heirs with Christ to the kingdom of God (Romans 8:17). As heirs of God we have an inheritance in His kingdom. Therefore, we are given authority in the kingdom of God. With our authority we can resist the devil and overcome the influence of sin in the flesh. Through our spiritual battles we are able to overcome principalities and powers of darkness, and pull down strongholds, arguments, and every high thing that exalts itself against the knowledge of God (2 Corinthians 10:4).

As heirs of God we have to authority to command the blessings of God in the land of the living because the things of God recognize our relationship with Christ. We are able to speak unseen things into existence and cancel the influence of things that work against the will of God. Our authority allows us to release our inheritance into the natural world according to our needs and some of our righteous desires.

We are also given the authority to be ambassadors for Christ in the world. We have been given the ministry of reconciliation, and God speaks through us to encourage others to reconcile to Him. As authorized speaking spirits we are able to release the things of God into our lives and the lives of others. We are able to speak life to people we influence and lead them into relationship with God through Christ Jesus.

If we are in Christ Jesus we are obligated to become new creations through the transformative power of His resurrection (2 Corinthians 5:17). We are obligated to love God with all our being and to love others as we love ourselves. The obligation of love becomes the sign of the new covenant that God has with humanity. We must demonstrate the kind of love that makes us obedient to God's commandments and committed to His service. We are required to present ourselves as living sacrifices to God with service that is holy and acceptable to Him. Our service must be given with gladness of heart and simplicity of spirit. We can't remain the same alienated creatures of darkness and death; rather we must be transformed as creations of light and life. We are transformed through our love, service, and commitment to honor God and bring glory to His name and His kingdom. Our power must be used according to the will of God, and the use of our authority must bring honor to God or that authority will be taken away and our power to influence will be diminished.

As empowered children of God and authorized heirs of the kingdom, we are obligated to give God the glory in honor, thanksgiving, and praise. Through our praise to God we demonstrate our understanding of what He has, is, and will do for us. We show our appreciation for God's goodness and become living billboards for God's message of spiritual renewal and transformation to a dying world. We also become signposts of inspiration for other believers to keep the faith and continue the good fight of faith, hope, and love. Our praise and honor also give us access to the power of God that operates within us (Romans 8:12-17).

The Bible instructs us that the abundant power of God is working in us beyond all that we could ask or imagine. The power of the resurrection is at work within us as God's children to separate us from sin and death, so that our lives give glory and honor to God (Ephesians 3:20). Through this power, God is using us to transform the world and preparing us to be with Him and to be like Him. The resurrection experience enables us to discard the old person of sin and death with its corrupt conduct of deceitful lusts. We become new creatures who walk as children of light in the holiness of God (Ephesians 4:17-24).

Chapter 20

Expressing the Resurrection

Sharing in Word

W hen you experience the resurrection of Jesus Christ you discover that it truly is a transforming experience. Part of that
transformation involves the need to share the experience with others
(Acts 1:8). The enlightenment gained from this experience provides
understanding of the connectivity of the human family. This enlightenment answers the age-old question of Cain by reminding us that
we are our brother's keeper and fills us with the desire to share our
experience with others (Genesis 4:9). The resurrection experience
gives us the willingness and the power to become witnesses of the
renewal, regeneration, and reconciliation of humanity to God. We
become witnesses of God's resurrection to the world in word and
deed, especially when we are actively involved in different forms
of worship.

As witnesses of the resurrection of Jesus Christ, we share in
word the good news of the gospel. We say something to the world of
the redemptive power of the gospel, which is the power of God unto
salvation (Romans 1:16). When we share this gospel, which contains the righteousness of God, He uses us to reveal His attributes to
those who are willing to believe. The attributes of God such as faith,
hope, and love separate us from the ungodliness and unrighteousness of humanity. In sharing the gospel, we share God and activate

His attributes within the believers, which separates them from sin and death. This is what is referred to as the activation of the Flaming Sword in our lives. The sharing process also activates and reinforces the attributes of God within the witnesses, helping them to remain separated from the sinful nature that abides within humanity.

The gospel is not at work in isolation, but rather the Holy Spirit is at work in connection with the Word in the lives of all believers. The Holy Spirit bears witness to the good news of the gospel and empowers the believer to serve as a witness to the entire world (Acts 1:8). The Holy Spirit gives life to the gospel we speak by becoming the spiritual witness to God's Word and connecting the power of God to our spoken word. The Holy Spirit connects us as witnesses to the presence of God and with each other. The Holy Spirit also enables us to remain separated from the things that hinder us from being in the presence of God. This is a necessary process in the fulfillment of divine purpose for our lives. Therefore God is active within our lives to draw us more and more into His presence and His reality.

Sharing in Deed

Because the death of Jesus atoned for all of our sins, our sharing of His resurrection makes us alive again to God. The Holy Spirit abides within us and connects us to God and Him to us (John 16:5-15). This abiding in the continuum of God allows us to take on the attributes of God. Our acceptance and willingness to operate in the nature and Spirit of God enables us to use the gifts of the Spirit He has given to His children. One of these gifts involves speaking life into the things of God. In witnessing to humanity we become instruments through which God shares Himself with those who are willing to listen and believe. As Jesus is the person of the Godhead responsible for atoning for our sins, the Holy Spirit is the person responsible for connecting us to God and one another.

In connecting believers to God, the Holy Spirit also empowers their actions and allows their deeds to become a witness of the resurrection power of Jesus. The Holy Spirit allows people to see God operating within the lives of believers. The life of the believer becomes a living testimony of the transformative power of resurrection. This transformation occurs as the Word of God and the Holy

Spirit interact to separate the believer from sinful habits and desires of the flesh and empowers them to operate in the nature of God. As people experience this transformation, they are encouraged to connect with God and remain in His connection.

Those who have experienced the resurrection power of God are transformed from sinners to children of God and are enabled to live as children of the light. As children of the light they reflect the nature of God to a world that is skewered in the darkness of sinful disobedience and ignorance of the righteousness of God (Ephesians 5:8-14). These living witnesses are instruments God uses to enlighten others who are trapped in the darkness of death and ignorance of God. Through the actions of believers God reveals Himself to humanity in an effort to awaken all to the knowledge of God. Those who are willing become living witnesses or gospel instruments that reflect the nature of God so that others may experience resurrection power. Jesus demonstrated this living witness and gospel instrument in His life as He informed and demonstrated to us the Father within Himself (John 14:7-11).

Jesus also indicated His desire for believers to share this experience of being one with the Father. Jesus' desire is illustrated in His promise of the Holy Spirit (Comforter) (John 14:15-18) and His prayer for humanity in the Garden of Gethsemane (John 17:20-26). The gospel of Jesus Christ is still being written in the lives of His believers, and people are still being saved through their testimonies of words and actions.

Sharing in Worship

Believers express their experience of the resurrection in their words to inform others and in their actions to inspire others. Believers also express their experience in worship, and while this type of expression informs and inspires others, believers are more interested in connecting with God. In worship, believers demonstrate their admiration, appreciation, and adoration for God. They admire Him for His power, sovereignty, and majesty in His mysterious and wonderful ways. They appreciate Him for His goodness, mercy, and compassionate involvement in their lives. They also adore Him for

His love and willingness to give so much that humanity can be with Him, and just for being God.

In worship, believers show admiration to God for His majesty and power. They express their awe of a God who is able to create worlds from nothing, keep the sun on schedule, cause the rain to fall on their fields, and allow the distant stars to sparkle in the darkness of space with the brilliance of their light. Believers witness the glory of God from the heavens and His handiworks in the firmament (Psalm 19:1). In wonder they celebrate His sovereignty over all and the mysterious ways in which He does it. In worship experiences words and deeds come together in expressions of love, faith, and thanksgiving toward God.

Appreciation is expressed by those who worship God for His goodness, mercy, and compassion. Worshippers understand that they are not good in themselves and it is the goodness of God operating within their lives that enables them to avoid the sinful and destructive tendencies of human nature. They know it was the acts of God working through Jesus Christ that saved them. Believers have a desire to show their appreciation for God through worship. Through sincere worship, believers are able to remove themselves from the pressures and pains of life. In the form of song, dance, prayer, preaching, and praise believers express their thanksgiving to God for keeping them in His presence.

The desire and need to connect with God draws believers into the worship experience. It is in worship that believers are able to connect with God and express their adoration for Him. This adoration or love of God can be described as a sincere desire to be with Him. In the praise and worship of God believers are drawn into His presence. The sanctuary becomes the throne room of God, the pulpit and altar becomes the throne, and the choir becomes the heavenly host of seraphim. The parishioners become the heavenly host of worshipers, the ministers become the elders who fall down and cast their crowns before His throne, while the praise leaders become the living creatures who cry "Holy, Holy, Holy, Lord God Almighty" (Revelation 4:1-11).

Through such experiences worshipers are able to transcend the natural limitations of sinful flesh and by the resurrection power of

Christ experience the presence of God. In these moments of connecting with God, old habits, desires, and natures die and allow room for God to infuse the essence of His holiness within the believer.

In worship the Word of God provides instruction of how to separate ourselves from the things that hinder our relationship with the Lord. Through this separation believers are allowed to enter into the presence of God and be informed by His Word. In worship believers begin to understand the purpose of being in God's presence, how to conduct themselves in the presence, and how to communicate with God and other believers. Understanding the Word of God enables us to speak the language of God and to interact on a personal level that is transformative and enlightening. Believers not only worship according to God's Word but with God's Word, and they receive the Word in worship that provides substance for living (the bread of life).

The Spirit of God provides connectivity in the worship experience. The Spirit allows natural sinful humans standing in a building on a troubled planet to transcend their natural surroundings and conditions so that they may enter the heavenly presence of a holy God. In these experiences, believers are transformed into creatures, who are able to share the resurrection experience with others. Upon entering the heavenly presence, those who worship God are connected with Him in ways that allow them to share existence with God. In connecting with God, believers are also able to connect with each other by the power of the Holy Spirit to become the family of God.

Chapter 21

Exemplifying the Resurrection

Understanding the Fellowship of His Suffering

In Jesus' crucifixion we discover His power to produce witnesses while fulfilling those things that were prophesied about His life. The amazing thing about the resurrection power of Jesus is that it began to work even before He died. Remember that Jesus said "If I am lifted up from the earth [not after I am dead] I'll draw all men unto me" (John 12:32). Jesus was able to influence people through His suffering, even before the completion of His purpose on earth.

The Scriptures illustrate a fellowship of His suffering that began to affect the people involved even as they experienced His persecution. We see the effect that Jesus' experience had on the wife of Pilate (Matthew 27:19) and even on Pilate himself (John 18:28-38). The Scriptures also illustrate a series of witnesses of the fulfillment of Jesus' purpose occurring near His death, at His death, and after His death. These witnesses were engaged in the suffering of Jesus and became part of the testimony of His triumph over sin and death.

Through the suffering of Jesus, believers are able to understand the power of self-denial and obedience. While Jesus was near death on the cross, as discussed earlier, one of the thieves noticed God within Him. Something manifested in Jesus on the cross that the thief did not see earlier, for he was also reviling Jesus (Mark 15:32). This thief became a witness of repentance while Jesus was drawing near to death. The repentant thief rebuked his fellow thief, confessed his sins, and calling Jesus Lord asked to be remembered in the kingdom. Jesus was so touched that He moved beyond the dispensation of time and promised the man paradise with Him the same day. This man exemplified the power of the resurrection by moving away from his past deeds and looking to a life with God beyond death. If we look beyond this life and death to an eternity with God, it will empower us to overcome the things that hinder us from God's will.

At death, the veil in the temple split from top to bottom signifying the removal of the separation of God and mankind. The veil became a witness of the invitation of humanity back into the presence of God. Because the veil split from top to bottom indicates that the invitation came from God. The veil became the witness of atonement (or "at-one-ment") as God opened the Holy of Holies to humanity. Through our relationship with Jesus we discover that the way into God's presence is open. Through this relationship we are drawn into the presence of God (John 12:32) and empowered to abide with Him (John 14:15-18).

After death the centurion saw God in the crucified Christ to the point of putting his life on the line to glorify God. This man became a witness of glorification and sent a signal to believers to glorify God regardless of the concern for earthly existence. From this witness we learn to operate our lives in a manner that brings glory to God and makes us not ashamed or afraid to announce our allegiance to Him in words and deeds. We become prepared to live our lives in a manner that glorifies God and overcome old allegiances of the flesh that hinder our relationship with God.

Leaving Things Behind

Through these three witnesses of the resurrection, we are able to understand that the power of the resurrection is about entering a new life where we leave old hindrances behind and move forward into a life and purpose with God. This testimony helps believers to understand that we reign with Him if we are willing to suffer with Him. At this point, believers are able to count former desires, accomplishments, and acquisitions that hinder relationship development with God as rubbish. We suffer the loss of our earthly selves to belong to God and abide in His presence. We become disciples of Christ through the fellowship of His suffering.

In suffering loss, we separate from the cursed things which are earthly and carnal in nature. As Jesus suffered death on the cross to gain atonement, reconciliation, and eternal life for humanity, we gain Christ in our loss. In gaining Christ we become prepared to use earthly gifts in our lives to the glory of God. We stop seeing our accomplishments and gains as the end of our means. Rather, we experience our accomplishments as acts of God through once broken vessels for inspiration to others. Earthly gains become tools in which God allows us to bless the kingdom. If our wealth can place food in the mouths of starving children, dig wells in drought-stricken areas, and give medical care to sick and dying people, then our wealth has given glory to God by edifying the kingdom. Jesus said whatever you do unto the least of these you do also unto Me (Matthew 25:37-40).

As disciples, we are prepared to move forward in our relationship with God, seeking the goal of the high prize in Christ Jesus, which is to be like Christ. Christ exemplified both divinity and humanity in a flawless manner. This is our goal, and Jesus is our example and our way to God. We strive to overcome and leave behind the things that prevent us from exemplifying God's divine nature in our natural existence. We have the love of God, the Spirit of God and the Word of God. The love of God enables us to move toward the heavenly prize. Knowing that we will not reach it on this side of life, we keep striving with the understanding that God will make the final separation through death or at the moment of the twinkling of an eye (1 Corinthians 15:52-55).

Through the blood of Jesus, our striving allows us to remain separated from the cursed things so that we are suitable for the presence and purpose of God (holy). We abide in God's presence where sin and death cannot abide. As we matriculate through this natural life, we experience the blessedness of belonging to God as His children. In belonging to God, we become conduits by which God blesses and transforms this existence to His will and purpose. We abide in a holy partnership with God as we help re-establish His holy kingdom on earth to the benefit of His creation, to the fulfillment of His purpose, and to the glory of His name.

Moving in Christ

The Scripture clearly indicates that we must keep striving even though we have not obtained what we seek (Philippians 3:12-16). We are instructed to press toward the upward call to be like Christ, who was the express image of God demonstrating the nature of the divine in His human existence. This is our goal and the divine purpose God is working to bring us to. The Scripture indicates that when Jesus appears in His divine glory, we shall see Him in a glorified manner and we shall be like Him (1 John 3:1-3). Therefore, we are expected to move from our lifestyles of stumbling in the darkness and become extensions of God from which He can illuminate and transform the lives of others. This was the purpose of Jesus' life on earth as He transformed the lives of all creation.

Remember that the resurrection power of Jesus had an influence on people before He finished His sacrifice and rose from the grave in victory. Therefore, we must allow God to use us as we strive toward perfection to influence others through the power of our testimonies. We are not to wait on perfection to make a difference, because perfection comes only after we die or when the Lord returns. We will not be able to help anyone then, or rather no one will need our help at that time. It is important that we use the time we have and the experiences we encounter to be an inspiration to others now. We were designed to influence the lives of others as we go through our experiences, be they good or bad.

The reason God is operating in our lives is to influence, inspire, and draw someone else to Himself. God can influence the lives of others through the testimonies of our experiences with Him. As others witness God's interventions in our lives and hear our word of testimony, God can transform their lives. If we are not in place or do not fulfill our purpose then someone could miss the witness of our testimony. This could hinder someone from receiving the inspiration that God planned for them and prolong their time of un-fulfillment and despair. The sharing of our testimony could be the reason that we give God to bless us through His miraculous power.

As a young man trying to answer my call into ministry, I remember thinking that I could find the way by myself. God sent a minister into my life who helped me to shift my focus from myself and the pleasures of life to seeking God's will for my life. He helped me through word, example, and testimony of his struggles how to draw near to God and allow God to release me from the bondages of fleshly desires. He also showed me how to listen and follow the voice of God in accepting and beginning to fulfill the purpose for which I was created.

After a couple of years God sent us in different directions, and he cared enough about me to come to my hometown to see that I was remaining with God in purpose. On a surprise visit to my hometown, he stopped to ask some people how to find me. Once he reached my house he did not stay long, but he shared with me that the people he spoke to told him about the work God was using me to do. He said he was satisfied and believed that I was with God, and he encouraged me to stay strong in the Lord. After he left I remember standing in the yard with my wife saying, "Thank You, Lord, for keeping me in Your will." I could not help wondering what if I had not remained faithful to my calling in my personal life.

About two years after Brother Miller's surprise visit, I called him one day. We had not talked in about five months at that time. His wife answered the phone and said he was not home but asked me to call him later; she knew he would be glad to hear from me. As instructed I called him later that night, and as we spoke I felt led to thank him for helping me to discover and accept my purpose in God. I went on to tell him how he helped to save my soul and that he helped to develop a soul winner for God. I told Brother Miller that as long as I served God the ministry God gave him would go on through me. I also told him that he would have a part in blessing everyone that God used me to bless because he touched my life.

Brother Miller listened to me but didn't say much, which was unusual for him, and soon after we hung up. The next night he called me to say thanks for our conversation. He informed me that because he had experienced some personal hurt from people close to him, he had stopped preaching. He had told God that he would not preach again, but my words the night before had reached him in ways that nothing else could. He said he asked God to forgive him after I shared my testimony and that he was walking in purpose again.

This knowledge moved me to the core of my existence. It deeply humbled me, leaving me to wonder what might have happened had I not obeyed God. I found it amazing that God used the very vessel that Brother Miller had helped to be there during his time of need. This situation also reminds me of our earthly vulnerabilities while inspiring me as to how wise God is and willing to intervene in our lives. God was working on Brother Miller's behalf before he had need of what God was preparing for him. God even used him to help prepare the instrument that He planned to use in his time of need. We must keep in mind that God knows all things past, present, and future, and He is able and willing to see us through.

We come to the point in our lives where we realize that we were saved and drawn to God through Christ so that we can become instruments of the resurrection power of Christ. We realize that our purpose in life involves influencing, inspiring, and leading others into relationship with Christ while giving glory to God through every aspect of our lives. As children of God we are His servants and instruments. We are no longer known according to our flesh, but rather we are known through our relationship with Christ. God has made us to be ambassadors through which He pleads with the world to be reconciled through Christ Jesus. This is the purpose of our earthly existence that God is empowering us to fulfill.

As believers and followers of God, we must allow His involvement in our lives to produce testimonies that draw and inspire witnesses of His goodness and salvation power. We must become like Jesus and exemplify the power of His resurrection in our human experiences. Through our victories and defeats we discover our strengths, overcome our fears, and build our fellowships of suffering (Philippians 3:10-11). In this process God will develop our testimonies and inspire witnesses of His power and love as He leads us to the fulfillment of divine purpose.

End Notes

Chapter 2: Understanding Demonic Influence

1. Crutcher, Mark E. The Flaming Sword, United States of America: Xulon Press, 2007, 33-36.

Chapter 9: Sword of Separation

2. Tillich, Paul. Systematic Theology Volume Two, Chicago: The University of Chicago Press, 1957, 10-11.

CPSIA information can be obtained at www.ICGtesting.com
Printed in the USA
LVOW091904071011

249449LV00002B/5/P